Political Risks
in International Business

Lars H. Thunell

The Praeger Special Studies program—
utilizing the most modern and efficient book
production techniques and a selective
worldwide distribution network—makes
available to the academic, government, and
business communities significant, timely
research in U.S. and international economic, social, and political development.

Political Risks in International Business

Investment Behavior of Multinational Corporations

PRAEGER SPECIAL STUDIES IN INTERNATIONAL BUSINESS, FINANCE, AND TRADE

Praeger Publishers   New York   London

332.673
T53p

Library of Congress Cataloging in Publication Data

Thunell, Lars H   1948-
   Political risks in international business.

   (Praeger special studies in international business,
finance, and trade)
   1. Investments, Foreign. 2. International business
enterprises. 3. Investments, Swedish. I. Title.
HG4538.T48   332.6'73   77-2940
ISBN 0-275-24500-4

Am

PRAEGER PUBLISHERS
200 Park Avenue, New York, N.Y. 10017, U.S.A.

Published in the United States of America in 1977
by Praeger Publishers, Inc.

789   038   987654321

Printed in the United States of America

ACKNOWLEDGMENTS

This book originated in 1972 during the time I was looking for a subject for my Ph.D. dissertation in political science at the University of Stockholm. I was educated in the tradition of classic theories of international politics and also had a strong interest in economics and business administration. But I found the academic fields of political science and economics both lacking in their treatment of the interrelationship between politics and economics. This is my attempt to bridge the gap between the two.

Writing this book has taken me on a long journey both in a physical and an intellectual sense. It started in the Political Science Department in Stockholm and ended at the Harvard Business School. As on all journeys, I have met many people, many of whom have been invaluable in my research. Especially I would like to thank my adviser Professor Kjell Goldmann of the University of Stockholm and the Swedish Center of International Affairs. He has given me total support especially at those times when I was in doubt as to what I was doing; he constantly urged me to clarify my concepts and improve my analysis.

Another source of inspiration was Professor Raymond Vernon of the Center for International Affairs and the Business School at Harvard. While I was a member of his seminar on International Business, he gave me many of the ideas that have been used in this book; the comments from him and other members of the seminar on an earlier draft of this book changed the course of the subsequent analysis. In addition, Professor Vernon in his capacity as project leader for the Multinational Enterprise project also allowed me to use the data bank created by him and the other researchers. Without that material my research would not have been possible.

The head of my department in Stockholm, Professor Olof Ruin, gave me encouragement and guidance both as a professor and a friend.

Other persons that have given me many suggestions and comments and to whom I wish to extend my thanks are Thomas Horst, Robert Kaufmann, Stephen Kobrin, Joseph Nye, Jr., Lars Otterbeck, Evert Vedung, Sverker Gustafsson, and Krister Wahlback. I want also to thank the many other people who have helped me. Most prominently, there were those at: the Department of Political Science, University of Stockholm; the Swedish Center of International Affairs; the Center for International Affairs at Harvard—where I spent a year and a half as research fellow—and the Harvard Business School.

I received programming help from the computer centers both at Harvard and in Stockholm. Bob Wymack of Harvard's Government Department spent many summer nights with me in 1975 trying to get the data in a format usable for my purposes. Julia Lunin helped me with some of the data collection, and

v

Kenje Gleason did a fantastic job typing several versions of the manuscript—especially when one considers my handwriting. Claes Linde helped me with the economic administration. I would also like to thank the business executives both in Sweden and the United States who took some of their valuable time to discuss the subject of political risk with me.

Furthermore I would like to thank my father for commenting on an earlier draft, my mother for typing the transcripts from the interviews, and both of them for providing me with the opportunity and encouragement to continue my education. And my wife Yvonne has been a wonderful companion on this long journey, helping and supporting me.

The research and my stay in the United States has been supported by scholarships and research grants from the University of Stockholm, the Royal Swedish Academy of the Sciences, the American-Scandinavian Foundation, and the Swedish Council for Social Science Research.

Finally, I take full responsibility for all that I have written.

CONTENTS

	Page
ACKNOWLEDGMENTS	v
LIST OF TABLES AND FIGURES	x

PART I: HYPOTHESES

Chapter

1	INTRODUCTION	3
	The Problem	3
	Political Risk	4
	Investment Climate	5
	Types of Political Risks	6
	Political Instability	7
	Measurement of Political Stability	10
	Hypotheses	13
	Other Modifications	14

2	THREE MODELS OF THE INVESTMENT DECISION	16
	The Unitary Actor Perspective	16
	Mature Oligopolies	17
	Other Economic Factors	19
	The Organizational Output Perspective	22
	The Decision Process	23
	Implications for this Study	25
	The Bureaucratic Model Perspective	27

3	OPERATIONALIZATION OF THE VARIABLES	29
	Political Instability Events	29
	Operational Definition of Investment	31
	Countries to Be Included in this Study	34
	Classification of Industries	35
	Degree of Oligopoly	35
	Labor Intensity	37
	Scale	37
	Country Profiles	37

PART II: TEST OF THE HYPOTHESES

4   ANALYSIS OF THE RELATIONSHIP   43

Regression Models   43
Changes in the Investment Trend   48
Result: Latin America   51
France, Spain, and Italy   55
Other Countries   58
Conclusions   60

5   ADDITIONAL EVIDENCE   65

Political Events—a Sufficient Condition for Change?   65
Relationships between Economic Indicators and
        Investment Flow   67
Importance of the Regime   68
Level of the Flow of Investments   70

6   DIFFERENCES BETWEEN TYPES OF INDUSTRIES
        AND MARKETS   72

Introduction   72
Scale   73
Labor Intensity   77
Degree of Concentration   79
Importance of Market Size   85
Conclusions   86

PART III: CONCLUSIONS

7   THEORETICAL CONCLUSIONS   89

Toward a Political Theory of Foreign Direct Investment   89
The Multinational Corporation as an Actor   91
    Is the Multinational Corporation an Actor?   92
    The Multinational Corporation as a Political Actor   94

8   NORMATIVE ASPECTS   96

Implications for Managers of Multinational
        Corporations   96
    Normative Statements   97
Political Risk Evaluation   98
    Strategies for Handling Political Risk   98

An Illustration: Kennecott in Chile   100
A Note on the Recent History of Takeovers   101
The Bargaining Game   101
Probability Estimation of Political Events   103
Earlier Models for Political Evaluation   104
Measurement of Political Instability   105
Conditions for Political Instability   107
Conclusions   109
Implications for Host-country Governments   110

APPENDIX A   111

APPENDIX B   112

APPENDIX C   114

APPENDIX D   119

APPENDIX E   122

REFERENCES   128

ABOUT THE AUTHOR   135

LIST OF TABLES AND FIGURES

Table		Page
3.1	Countries Included in the Analysis	36
3.2	Country Profiles: Investments by U.S. and European Companies, 1948–67	38
4.1	Pearson Correlation between Changes in the Number of Subsidiaries Established and Deaths in Political Violence, Latin America, 1949–67	46
4.2	Ratios between Years of Trend Change and of No Change: U.S. Investments in Mexico, Brazil, and Argentina	52
4.3	Ratios between Years of Trend Change and of No Change: European Investments in Mexico, Brazil, and Argentina	54
4.4	Ratios between Years of Trend Change and of No Change: U.S. Investments in France, Spain, and Italy	56
4.5	Ratios between Years of Trend Change and of No Change: European Investments in France, Spain, and Italy	57
4.6	Ratios between Years of Trend Change and of No Change: Summary Table	62
5.1	Investments in Years of Maximum Violence	66
5.2	Pearson Correlation between some Economic Indicators and the Number of Subsidiaries Established	69
5.3	Step-wise Regression Equation of the Average Number of Investments during the Periods between Trend Changes	71
6.1	Differences between Investments in Large-scale and Small-scale Industries in Mexico, Brazil, and Argentina	74
6.2	Differences between Investments in Large-scale and Small-scale Industries in France, Spain, and Italy	75
6.3	Differences between Investments in High and Low Labor-intensity Industries in Mexico, Brazil, and Argentina	78

6.4   Differences between U.S. Investments in High and Low
       Labor-intensive Industries in Mexico   80

6.5   Differences between Investments in High and Low
       Labor-intensive Industries in France, Spain, and Italy   81

6.6   Differences between Investments in High and Low
       Concentration Industries in Mexico, Brazil, and Argentina   83

6.7   Differences between Investments in High and Low
       Concentration Industries in France, Spain, and Italy   84

6.8   Differences between U.S. Investments in Large and Small
       Markets   86

A.1   Pearson Correlation between Different Measures of
       Investment Flows   111

C.1   Classification of Industries   114

D.1   Step-wise Regression Equations for Latin America   119

D.2   Step-wise Regression Equations for Europe and Africa   120

D.3   Step-wise Regression Equations for Asia   121

E.1   Factor Solutions for Latin America   122

E.2   Factor Solutions for Colombia   123

E.3   Factor Solutions for Venezuela   124

E.4   Factor Solutions for Argentina   125

E.5   Factor Solutions for Chile   126

E.6   Factor Solutions for Brazil   127

Figure

2.1   The Investment-Decision Process   25

4.1   Number of Subsidiaries Established in Brazil, 1948–67   44

4.2   U.S. and European Cumulative Investments in Brazil,
       1948–67   49

HYPOTHESES

1

INTRODUCTION

THE PROBLEM

Some foreign companies are now hesitating to invest in Italy and many of the companies who already have operations in that country are trying to sell them or just close them. This is one example of how enterprises, especially big multinational ones, react to political disturbances and changes in their environment. Lebanon, Portugal, Chile, and so on, are other examples where similar things have happened. The question can be raised whether there is any pattern in the way companies react to political changes and if every company reacts in the same fashion. The term react means here investment behavior and changes in it. A company can, of course, react in many other ways. The behavior of the International Telephone and Telegraph (ITT) Corporation in Chile under and before Allende is one example of a different type of reaction. Another is the recent disclosures of bribes by companies to government officials.

The aim of this study is to analyze if and if so how the investment decisions of large multinational enterprises are influenced by political events in the potential host country. In reality one can probably find an influence in the other direction too; that is, political events in a country may be influenced by changes in the flow of foreign investment into that country. This is something that will not be analyzed here.

It is hoped that the knowledge generated by this study will have both theoretical and practical value. In the concluding chapters the theoretical implications for the academic fields of international relations and international economics will be discussed. What normative implications this study has for decision makers both in the governments of the concerned countries and in the managements of the investing corporations will also be considered. This will be done not only by looking at the result here, but also by broadening the perspective and looking at some of the literature in both business administration and political science.

POLITICAL RISK

The importance of political events can probably best be analyzed within the framework of political risk evaluation. Robock defined political risk in international business as existing when: (1) discontinuities can occur in the business environment; (2) these discontinuities are difficult to anticipate; (3) and are the result of political change (Robock 1971, p. 7). "To constitute a risk these changes in the business environment must have a potential for significantly affecting the profit or other goals of a particular enterprise." (Robock 1971, p. 7). This means that the political change has to be relevant to the corporation to constitute a risk. The risk can be of a relevant change anywhere in the environment, the home country, the host country, or a third country; it can also be of a change in the relationship between any pair of countries. Examples of the latter are wars and trade and currency agreements. An example of a political risk in the home country is the demand for, and thus a chance for, regulation of foreign investments. This study will be limited to political changes in the host countries.

When discontinuities occur in the environment, they can of course affect each corporation differently. Some companies might take advantage of them, while others receive a disadvantage. The formation of the European Common Market was, for example, an event that had negative consequences for companies that earlier were protected behind the tariff barriers, such as French manufacturers of refrigerators. But at the same time this event had positive consequences for many companies; many American companies, for example, could take advantage of the larger market. When political risk is discussed there is a tendency to do this only by reference to the possible negative consequences rather than by also seeing the new possibilities that can open up through political events.

The political changes have to be difficult to anticipate to constitute a political risk according to Robock's definition. This means that the change may not be gradual and easy to forecast; instead it must go in another direction or occur at another time than was anticipated.

A distinction between risk and uncertainty must also be made here. When the decision maker has full information about the objective probabilities for all possible outcomes, then there is a risk for a certain outcome, but when he does not know the objective probabilities, or even all the possible outcomes, then uncertainty is at hand. Except perhaps for the most simple decisions, it is in reality always the latter case that exists. But decision makers often act as if there were objective probabilities. The different outcomes are given subjective probabilities based on intuition or a more strictly done evaluation (Aharoni 1966, p. 17).

> When the international manager makes a judgment of an uncertain political event in a host country he thereby converts a political uncertainty into political risk (Root 1972, p. 57).

Through more information the evaluation of the subjective risk can be better based and thus the uncertainty reduced. This information has a cost; the decision maker has to make a trade off between this and the value of the reduction in uncertainty.

According to Robock's definition the discontinuities have to stem from political change to constitute a political risk. One of the most common definitions of politics is "the authoritative allocation of values" (Easton 1965). Political changes are thus those factors that are not related to any supply and demand relations, that is, to a market. It is still very hard to differentiate between the two. First, since economies are dependent upon politics, politics determines the regime, that is, the rules, for the economic interactions. Second, political decisions are often made out of economic necessity. This is especially true in the long run. Even if the borderline is hard to draw, this gives a good starting point when trying to evaluate if a possible change constitutes a political or economic risk. To sum up this section, Robock has been followed and political risk has been defined as existing when unanticipated discontinuities affecting the corporation resulting from political changes can occur in the business environment.

INVESTMENT CLIMATE

From the discussion above it is clear that political risk is the risk of changes. It is, for example, possible changes in the rules for foreign investment that constitute the risk, not the rules themselves. Very often in the analysis of political risk, however, the political uncertainty of a particular country is mixed with the policy in that country toward foreign investment, that is, the regime for foreign investment. The term often used for the latter is "investment climate." According to the traditional use of this term, a country can have a bad investment climate for two reasons: either because of the policy itself, or because there is great uncertainty about the stability of that policy regardless of whether it is good or bad.

Different authors have used the concept of investment climate in different ways. Stobaugh shows one company's evaluation model where the following variables are included: foreign ownership allowed, discrimination and controls, stability of domestic prices, political stability, willingness to grant tariff protection, availability of local capital, and currency stability (Stobaugh 1969a,

p. 132; 1969b, p. 102). As one can see from this list, investment climate includes some variables that describe the current situation and others like political stability that really are indicators of the uncertainty, or risk for a change, of the current rules.

Other writers use a still broader definition of investment climate. The Organization for Economic Cooperation and Development (OECD) has in one study also included infrastructure and bureaucracy (OECD 1968, p. 8). One of the broadest definitions is used by Nehrt. He describes a country's investment climate as having different parts: economic climate A, the current economic situation and tendencies; economic climate B, the institutional structure and infrastructure; social climate, for example, working conditions; administrative climate, for example, red tape; and political climate, which is risk for nationalizations or expropriations, change of regime, or revolution (Litvak and Maule 1970, pp. 304–06).

Behind the use of investment climate in the way described above there seems to be an assumption that the harder the conditions are for foreign investment, the greater is the risk for actions against the companies in the form of new regulations. In some cases this is probably true, for example when there is a trend towards stiffer regulation of foreign investment. But one could easily find examples and situations when this is not true. Some countries have very strict regulations on foreign investment, but the probability for new regulations or nationalization is very low. In this case the situation is not uncertain; it is just regulated.

From this discussion it should be clear that analyses of the current situation often are mixed with prospects for the future without differentiating between the two. It is very important to understand political risk and investment climate as two different things. The following quotation from the president of one of the biggest manufacturing companies in Sweden illuminates this point very well:

> ... what the characteristics are of the regime in power at the moment, that is not especially important. The important thing is that the company within certain limits can predict the development in that country.*

TYPES OF POLITICAL RISKS

As mentioned above, this study is limited to political changes within the host countries. When discussing types of political risks we will therefore make the same limitation, but we should not forget that there are many other types of political risks, for example, the relationship between countries.

---

*Source: personal interview data, see note, p. 15.

In the host country a company can be affected by two main types of political changes: changes in the regime under which it operates or changes in the political stability of the country. The regime is defined as the rules under which the economy, including foreign companies, works in the country. On different levels of abstraction these rules consist of the ideology of the government, the generalized policy, and how this policy is applied.

There are two types of political stability that seem to be relevant: stability at the grassroots level in the periphery of the society, here called "mass political stability," and stability in the center of the society, here called "government political stability." Examples of the first type are riots, demonstrations, and political strikes; examples of the latter are changes of government, coups, and so on. The two types are of course dependent upon each other. Mass political instability is often followed by changes in the government, and a change of government is often accompanied by mass instability.

Independent of the level of society it occurs on, instability can affect a corporation in at least two different ways: directly and indirectly. On the center level, companies are directly affected because government instability is often accompanied by administrative paralysis, and earlier decisions are often reexamined. One Swedish executive said that when his company established a subsidiary in Brazil, they had to negotiate with three different governments. A company can also be directly affected by mass political instability (Robock 1971, p. 12). One recent example of this is Portugal where many company facilities were occupied by workers.

Companies are indirectly influenced because disturbances at any level are often followed by changes in the regime under which the companies operate. In the extreme negative case the companies are forced to leave the country, if, for example, they are nationalized. That this can happen after instability at the government level, and especially after a government transfer, is hardly surprising, but it is not uncommon after mass instability either, since demonstrations are often directed towards foreign interests in the country. Even if this is not the case, the government often tries to use the foreign interests as a scapegoat to save itself.

Finally, a distinction should be made between changes that are directed towards all companies, and especially perhaps all foreign corporations, and changes that are directed only toward a few corporations with certain characteristics. Robock calls this macro- and micro-political risk (Robock 1971, p. 9).

POLITICAL INSTABILITY

Possible changes in the political stability of a country constitute a political risk, as has been seen above. The problem is, however, that even if the current political stability can be measured and estimated, it is very hard to know how this will affect political stability in the future. This means that it is extremely difficult to estimate political risk. Political scientists have done some research in this area, which will be discussed in Chapter 8, but this problem has not been systematically studied within most corporations.

Quite a few interview-studies of company executives show that political risk is considered as one of the most important factors when a company is deciding whether or not to invest in a foreign country. Root, for example, writes that his interviews with "these executives revealed that market opportunity and political risk are the dominant factors in most investment decisions" (Root 1968, p. 74). Aharoni finds the same thing: the country must first and foremost show economic and political stability (Aharoni 1966, p. 93, p. 100). Swansb-rough found in his analysis of American executives' views of nationalism in Latin America that "restrictive economic policies" and "political instability" were the two most serious problems confronting an American investor (Swansbrough 1972, p. 68). Similar results have been obtained by Stonehill and Nathanson (1968, p. 49), Stobaugh (1969b, p. 103), Reuber (1973, p. 94), *Fortune* (1968), the National Industrial Conference Board (1969, p. 3), and *Business International* (1968, p. 25).

Paradoxically, however, these studies also show that systematic analysis and evaluations of these risks are rarely done. According to Root: "Regardless of their investment strategies American companies do not appraise political risk abroad in a formal systematic way " (1968, p. 76). Aharoni writes:

> The risk talked about is that presumed to exist. These presumptions are based on a general image of a specific country, of a whole continent, of less developed countries as a whole, or even of foreign countries in general. Risk is not described in terms of the impact on a specific investment. It is rather described in general terms and stems from ignorance, generalizations, projections of U.S. culture and standards to other countries, and an unqualified deduction from some general indicator to a specific investment (1966, p. 94).

And Piper states that:

> The decision maker, by virtue of habit, custom and training is prone to analyze the foreign investment within the same framework as previous domestic invest-ments, utilizing the same assumptions, analytic tools and intuitions that have brought investment success in the considerably less complicated domestic envi-ronment (Piper 1971, p. 12).

This means that the decision maker often uses current political stability as an indicator of the risk for changes either in the stability or in the regime. In practice it is probably a rather good indicator; theoretically, however, as the figure below shows, one can distinguish between different combinations of the relationship between current and future political stability.*

The aim of this study is to measure political instability as a part of political risk and to analyze the relationship between that and the outcome of the investment decision process. By doing this it should be possible to draw some conclusions on how political instability and thus political risks affect investment decisions. There are of course also many other factors besides political risks that influence the decision process; many of these factors probably influence it more. These will be discussed in Chapter 2.

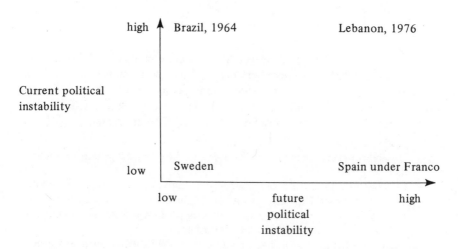

From earlier research in this area by Kobrin (1975, pp. 13–20) and Green (1972, pp. 62–83) it is known that there seems to be no relationship between the book value of investments made and the degree of political stability. There were even no relationships found between the flow of investments during a specific year and the stability that year, according to a cross-sectional study done by Kobrin.[†] This means that the effect of political instability on how investments are allocated between countries is very limited in the short run. But this does not exclude the possibility that the degree of political stability can have great influence on how the investments are allocated over time in a given country. It is thus necessary to focus on the relationship over time in a given country between political instability and investments.

---

*This is thus a problem of validity for the decision maker, and hence for this study.
[†]*Source:* personal conversation.

MEASUREMENT OF POLITICAL STABILITY

So far political instability has been discussed in general terms, but it has not been defined nor have ways it can be measured been shown. In a survey of the political science literature on political stability, Hurwitz (1973, pp. 449–63) found five approaches that had been used to define political stability:

1. The absence of violence and disturbance
2. Government longevity/endurance
3. The existence of a legitmate constitutional order
4. The absence of structural change
5. Combinations of 1 to 4, that is, a multifaceted approach.

In recent political science research the concept of political stability has been broadened to what the researchers call political performance. Eckstein has argued that this concept has four dimensions. As seen below, these dimensions are very similar to the approaches found by Hurwitz and thus political performance as a concept is very similar to Hurwitz' fifth approach:

1. Durability [is] persistence of a polity over time. The longer it persists the higher its performance.
2. Civil order [is] the absence of unregulated collective resorts to violence (or acts in which violence is overtly threatened or for other reasons very likely) to achieve private or public objectives. Polities perform well to the extent that such actual or latent violence does not occur.
3. Legitimacy [is] the extent that a polity is regarded by its members as worthy of its support. A polity performs well to the extent that it is so regarded.
4. Decision efficacy [is] the extent to which polities make and carry out prompt and relevant decisions in response to political challenges. The greater is efficacy, the higher is performance (Eckstein 1973, pp. 21, 32, 50, and 65).

There are a few weaknesses connected with these dimensions which became really noticeable when Gurr tried to operationalize them (Gurr and McClelland 1971, pp. 10–63). Durability is then defined as the number of years the polity existed, and thus becomes the result of how well the polity performs in the other dimensions. Legitimacy is operationally defined as the amount of open protest. This means that legitimacy comes very close to civil order. There can also be different "objects of legitimacy: the political community, the regime, its incumbents, and its policies." Decision efficacy is operationalized by Gurr through studying two key areas, budget allocation and maintenance of authority.

Studying the relationships between these variables Gurr finds the following model (Gurr and McClelland 1971):*

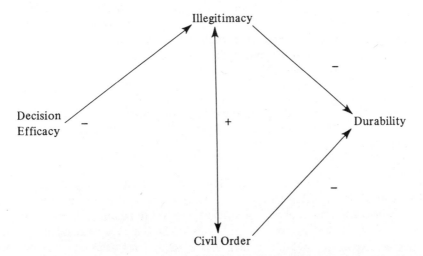

There are thus two things that make it very hard to distinguish between the dimensions. The indicators measure partly the same thing and they are causally related. It is clear that the key dimension is civil order, which means that nonoccurrence of violence and disturbance is the core in a multifaceted approach to political stability and thus the dimension on which to focus. On the other hand the problems connected with this approach must not be forgotten. Measuring just overt violence, while forgetting about latent instability as well as the country's ability to tolerate disturbances, for example through a strong institutionalization, can result in questionable conclusions.

Nevertheless, it is now possible to define political stability as the absence of disturbances and violence in the society. It has been seen earlier that there are two main groups of disturbances tha· are relevant for investing companies: government disturbances and mass political disturbances.

A condition for using this approach is that there must be some regularities in the society; otherwise we cannot speak of disturbances. In sociological terms one can say that the society is built upon roles. These roles are patterns of behavior. Because there are expectations in the environment as to how a person

---

*The arrows imply causal relationships. A positive sign means that when one variable increases (decreases), the other increases (decreases) too. A negative sign means that when one variable increases (decreases) the other decreases (increases).

in a specific role shall behave, the behavior is not random but has a specific pattern. The role limits the individual's behavior. This makes it possible to predict the individual's behavior and it also makes it possible to speak of disturbances when a person does not do as expected in that role. According to this view, the political structure is the pattern of interactions with political content between different roles. Political stability is thus the regularity in this pattern. The more regularity, the more stability.

> We might say that there is political stability to the extent that members of society restrict themselves to the behavior pattern imposed by role expectations (Ake 1975, p. 273)

What types of disturbances should be included when we analyze the political stability? Ake says that all types should be included. But this is not possible in reality, so a way of choosing certain types has to be found. Some hints can be obtained by looking at the aim of this study, which is to analyze how the degree of political stability influences a corporation's decision to invest; the changes, that is, disturbances, thus have to be relevant to the companies. Furthermore, a person's expectations of other individuals' behavior are a function of his value system, earlier experience, and so on. It is almost certain that a decision maker in a big corporation has been brought up and had his education and professional training in one of the industrialized countries in the West. This means that his expectations and values probably have their point of reference in those countries. It has also been seen above that there is seldom a systematic analysis of the country in which the company is considering an investment. Instead, the decision is often built upon the intuition of the decision maker. This means that all events in the potential host country which are unusual in the industrialized countries will probably be viewed as disturbances and signs of political instability, even if they are part of the political culture and tradition.

When political stability is measured, a number of events should be used that can constitute disturbances and so increase the political risk. The political instability and the political risk is high when the frequency of the events is high. The events to be analyzed and the data base to be used will be described in Chapter 3. Also discussed there will be how the different events can be aggregated together to get one measure of government political stability and another of mass political stability. Note that the empirical analysis will concern the relationship between "objective" political instability and investments. The decision maker and thus the "subjective" stability is only a link between the two. The discussion above can thus be said to concern the validity of the measures.

HYPOTHESES

Which events affect corporations, that is, which events increase political risk and thus influence the behavior of the investing corporations? Are there any differences between types of host countries? Between different types of companies? These are the types of questions that this study will attempt to answer.

In a very generalized form it will here be assumed that international business executives are weighing the return of investment, both in absolute and relative terms, versus risks, of which political risk is one. Given a certain rate of return, the investments will therefore decrease when the political risk is high and vice versa. Most of the hypotheses that will be stated in this chapter and the next will only be specific cases of this general hypothesis.

The investments are a flow, which means that they will be measured as an amount per year. The big question then is, using decrease in the hypothesis above, do we mean that the absolute level shall be lowest during years of high political risk or the decrease, the change, will be largest. Arguments for or rather against both are easy to find. We will use the change in investment flow as the dependent variable, since the relationship between changes and risk is probably more direct than the relationship between risk and the absolute level of investment. The decrease in investment shall thus be larger the higher the political risk and vice versa.

The first and basic hypothesis specifies the importance of political instability:

Hypothesis 1:
The investments in a country decrease when a country is unstable and increase when it is stable, ceteris paribus.

This hypothesis must be modified on a whole set of points. In this section a few of these will be discussed, and in the following chapters different types of companies and countries will be discussed separately.

As mentioned above, one main problem is that company executives not only have a yes-no choice, they can also increase the rate of return demanded for profits in a certain area or country and thus ask for a premium for risk. But this will probably not level out all changes in the investment flows since the number of potential projects probably decreases the higher rate of return demanded (Reuber 1970, p. 94, 98; Stobaugh 1969b, pp. 101–06; Carlsson 1969, p. 119f).

Second and perhaps more important, is something that also has been discussed earlier: Some events may have stabilizing effects, even if they themselves constitute disturbances. For example, the consequence of Suharto's coup in Indonesia was a stabilization of the situation there and a tremendous improvement of the investment climate. For analytical reasons it is preferred to distingush events from their effects; the events as such are here viewed as destabilizing although their consequences can be a change of policy that is positive to the companies. The problem is that when the effect of a disturbance on the investment of some companies is studied, it is found that—due to the change in policy—the disturbance will be followed by increasing investment instead of decreasing investment as hypothesis 1 says. This is probably more relevant to government events than to mass disturbances for obvious reasons. If the government disturbance is followed by a change in investment climate that is positive for foreign investors, then these investments will increase, probably significantly. One can therefore hypothesize that after some government events there will be an increase in the investment flow instead of a decrease.

Hypothesis 2:
Government events will be followed either by an increase or a decrease in investment, in both cases of a larger size than after mass political events.

Another caveat has to do with the temporal sequences of the variables. In this study the political instability in a certain country is the independent variable and the investment of some companies in that country is the dependent variable. When testing the hypotheses the covariance between variables will be studied. If a covariance is found, this is an indication that the causal relationship we have discussed on a theoretical level might exist. But for a relationship to be causal, changes in the independent variable must logically precede changes in the dependent variable. In this case, however, one must remember that the independent variable really is an approximation of another variable: the expectations of political stability. It could therefore happen that the expected changes already are "discounted" when they actually happen, and a reverse time-order is obtained. This should not happen too often though, because the trend probably has to be very obvious before the companies discount it. But there are cases when anybody can see that the country is heading towards political instability. One example of this is Argentina at the end of Frondizi's government, when the foreign investment flow decreased rapidly before the coup against him. If it is possible for the business executive to see the change, however, one should also be able to see it with the measuring instruments used here.

OTHER MODIFICATIONS

In the following chapter three approaches to analyzing decision making and the implications these have for the basic hypothesis will be discussed.

The three approaches, which are complementary, are common in economic literature as well as in the literature of political science (Allison 1971). The border between them is blurred, but since they are only used here to generate hypotheses, there is no reason to try to draw an exact border line.

According to the first approach or perspective, one looks upon the decision process as one single decision being made by one unitary actor, which can be a company or country. The actor has certain goals, and he uses his resources rationally to achieve these goals. In the second perspective, one no longer looks upon the company as a unit. Instead it is seen as an organization in which there is a decision process that goes on according to rules and routines. Organizational theory is obviously central to this approach. In the third approach, the decision is the result of a power play within the bureaucracy constituting the organization.

All these models deal with rationality. In the first it is the organization as a whole that acts rationally. In the second, routines are used because the realities are so complex that one cannot take everything into consideration and because the decision is a process with many people involved. In the third model the different groups act rationally because they are forwarding their own interests, and what they believe is right for the organization as a whole.

With the help of these three perspectives different theories about the investment decision process will be examined in order to modify the basic hypothesis. For this some of the literature in the field has been reviewed and also some interviewing with executives in seven Swedish multinationals has been done.* The aim of the interviews was to try to identify variables that were thought to be relevant within the companies and to improve our own understanding of the complex decision making process. Of course these interviews are of little direct scientific value, but they are useful for clarification. Since the interviewed persons were promised confidentiality, no references to persons or companies are made.

---

*One chairman, two presidents, two vice-presidents of corporate planning, one vice-president for administration, one vice-president for public affairs and one vice-president for special assistance to the president were interviewed. They came from the following companies: AGA, Alfa Laval, Electrolux, L.M.Ericsson, SKF, Svenska Tandsticks AB (Swedish Match), and Volvo. Each interview was about an hour long. One was made by telephone, the rest at personal meetings. They were open and could be characterized as discussions where the interviewer (the author) had a list of subjects to be raised. The interviews were done in Swedish and quotes are translated to English by the author.

2

THREE MODELS
OF THE INVESTMENT
DECISION

THE UNITARY ACTOR PERSPECTIVE

Most writers discussing foreign investment agree that foreign investment to a large extent is a function of market imperfections. Hymer was one of the first to systematically analyze monopoly power as an explanation for foreign investment (Hymer 1976), but he has had many followers.

Vernon has discussed the effect of multinational companies on the location of economic activities (Vernon 1974, pp. 89–114). He starts out with the observation that most multinational enterprises are active within industries that are characterized by oligopoly. Which base the oligopoly has will have some consequences for how the company will behave. The argument for this is built upon Vernon's own product-cycle theory. According to this a product goes through a cycle of initiation, exponential growth, slowdown, and decline. The production and market conditions differ depending on which stage the product is in.

During the first stage the product is manufactured in short series, the price is high, and the market small. The company has some monopoly on the technology. But the production or the production process becomes standardized at the same time as the price goes down; thus the product can be manufactured and sold in larger quantities. This in turn means that it becomes easier for competitors to enter and start production. A similar effect occurs when the company starts to export the product. At a certain point it becomes more profitable to use local manufacturing, especially since the company may have to do so to head off and compete with local companies. The triggering factor to start local manufacturing is very often, especially in the developing countries, a raise in tariffs, or a threat of higher tariffs (Vernon, 1971, pp. 66–77) at the same time as some companies are "invited" to start production by the government.

Under the first stages of the product cycle the oligopoly is based upon knowledge and exclusive technology. Vernon calls this innovation based oligopolies. During this time local production is relatively seldom established abroad. When the shift happens depends on different factors:

> ... the answer to this question turns on various elements. First, there is the question of factor costs; in case of U.S.-based producers, labor-intensive products are earlier candidates for a defensive shift in the location of production facilities than are capital-intensive products, simply because of the high cost of labor in the United States. Then there is the question of scale; products with relatively small economies of scale in production are sooner established abroad than those with large. In addition, where transportation costs and barriers at the border are relatively high, the decision to serve foreign markets from local facilities is indicated sooner (Vernon 1974, p. 95).

Looking at Swedish companies one can clearly see the effect of the small home market: they establish subsidiaries abroad very early relative to American companies.

Mature Oligopolies

During the second half of the product life cycle the facilities for production abroad are established. The technology is now more easily accessible to everybody. According to Vernon this does not mean, however, that the period of oligopoly is necessarily over.

> If scale economies in production or marketing have meanwhile become very important, they may replace the innovation factor as a major barrier to entry. In that case, the industry will have evolved to the state of what I shall call a "mature oligopoly" (Vernon 1974, p. 96).

This type of oligopoly is thus common in large-scale industries, and in sales-promotion-intensive industries.

That oligopolistic behavior to a large extent can explain the establishment of production abroad has been shown by Federick T. Knickerbocker in his study of the same 187 U.S. based multinationals that we will study (Knickerbocker 1973). His results show that when one company establishes production in a country the other companies in the oligopoly are quick to follow. They want to guard themselves against every possible threat to the stability of the oligopoly. How soon the other companies react depends on the degree of oligopoly in the industry and the stability of the oligopoly. But it also depends on how important the market is for the companies and how important it might become, that is, the less diversified the companies are, by product or geography, the sooner they follow; the larger the market or market growth, the faster the reaction. Economy of scale puts a restriction on the response so that only the leading companies react.

Knickerbocker also shows that variation in the reaction between host countries is primarily explained by an index of Political stability. The reaction is stronger the more stable the country is (Knickerbocker 1973, p. 171ff.).* There are, however, some serious methodological problems with this index and the way Knickerbocker uses it. Therefore a test of Knickerbocker's result was made. Instead of the index, its different parts were used: ethno-linguistic fragmentation, number of people dead in political violence, and the time the country had been a sovereign state.†

The result of this reanalysis indeed shows that those variables seem to be of great importance for the oligopolistic reaction. Their explanatory power is, however, not as great as Knickerbocker finds it. Further, the political variables seem to be more important for the short-term reaction than for the long-term reaction, which supports the results obtained by Green and Korbin doing cross-sectional analysis of investment stocks and political stability (Green 1972, pp. 62–83; Korbin 1975, pp. 13–20).

We are now able to formulate the following hypothesis:

---

*Knickerbocker's index of the oligopolistic reaction is built in the following way: As base data Knickerbocker used the data collected on 187 U.S.-based multinationals by the Harvard Business School Multinational Enterprise Project. For 21 countries, for every two-digit type of industry according to the S.I.C. classification, and for every year from 1948–67, he counted the number of manufacturing subsidiaries established by the 187 companies. From every time series he got, he chose the 3-, 5- and 7-year periods during which most of the establishment had been done. He then determined what portion of all the establishments in a particular country and industry had been done during these periods. Then by averaging the values of the industries for every country, Knickerbocker got his three indices of oligopolistic reaction per country (Knickerbocker 1973, p. 34ff.).

†The political instability index was built by Sherbini and is a summation of the three variables mentioned in the text (Liander 1967). The problem with Sherbini's index is, however, that it is built in such a way that the countries can only get the values 1-10 (that is, 0-100 with only even 10ths used). The result of this is that many of the 21 countries included in Knickerbocker's analysis are assigned the same value. For this reason it is not surprising that this index gets such explanatory power in Knickerbocker's regression equations. In the analysis a number of variables were taken from the *World Handbook of Political and Social Indicators,* aggregate data file (1972). This data collection was also the source for Sherbini's data. Years of sovereignty never showed up in the equations; neither did political deaths, the latter probably because that variable is highly skewed. Instead, riots was included into the step-wise regressions. This variable is highly correlated with political deaths but more evenly distributed.

Hypothesis 3:
   The higher the degree of oligopoly in the industry in which the company
   is, the weaker the relationship between political stability and foreign investment.

Other Economic Factors

There are some industries which are not oligopolistic, but are instead much
more similar to the small company in classic economic theory. Those companies are influenced by some economic factors that will be discussed below. But
one must remember, as Vernon pointed out in the quotation above, that the
companies in an oligopoly are not free from these factors. For example, a
company can get an advantage in the competition with the other companies
by following the Hecher-Olin factor theory and producing where the factor
costs are lowest.

There are different types of economic factors that influence the companies.
If the assumption is made that the companies want to maximize their profit
or their growth, some factors can be found that influence the companies'
behavior. The evaluation of an investment project must in this case be an
analysis where possible costs and benefits are weighed against each other. For
example, the bigger the chance for good profits and growth, the lesser the
importance of a small risk, that is, political instability. This means that the
larger the market and/or its growth in a country, the weaker the relationship
between the political stability and the foreign investment in that country,
assuming that big markets and growth markets are perceived as being more
profitable. This is the fourth hypothesis.

Hypothesis 4:
   The larger the market and/or market growth a country has, the weaker the
   relationship, ceteris paribus, between political stability and foreign direct
   investment in that country.

For the importance of the cost of production factors the argument is in
principle the same as above, although in this case the substitutability of the
production factors between countries has to be taken into account. The easier
it is to substitute production factors in one country for those in another, the
more sensitive are the companies in that industry to political instability.

The production factor that is important for foreign investment in the type
of country discussed here is labor. Many investments in the developing countries are made to take advantage of the cheap labor cost, but it is not very
important in which country this is done, since the product is often exported.
It can thus be hypothesized that the more the investment is made to exploit

cheap labor cost, the more sensitive the company is to changes in political stability. Assuming that labor costs are more important in highly labor-intensive industries, the following hypothesis is obtained:

Hypothesis 5:
   The relationship between investments and political stability is stronger, ceteris paribus, for companies in highly labor-intensive industries than for companies in industries that are not labor-intensive.

Raw materials are very interesting in this context because the companies exploiting raw materials are forced to be where the raw materials are. Even if they refine them elsewhere they have to be extracted. Following the same argument as above, the conclusion can be drawn that companies in those industries are relatively less sensitive to changes in political stability. But in this case it is also possible to argue the complete opposite: extractive industries are often the first to be hit by political events, and therefore the companies in those industries are relatively more sensitive to political instability. This argument is underlined by the fact that extractive industries are very large scale and hence the potential losses greater.

Since only manufacturing industries are analyzed in the empirical part of this study, no hypothesis will be stated but one should remember and be aware of the importance of raw material for manufacturing industries too.

One thing that clearly influences the substitutability between countries is the relative economic distance between the places of possible production and the market. Economic distance is used here to mean not only transport costs but also tariffs and other trade barriers. If the economic distance is small, it is easier to substitute production in one country for that in another; the sensitivity to political instability will be high. The economic distance can vary both by industry and pair of countries. This hypothesis will not be tested because of the huge problems involved in operationalizing economic distance, but again one should be aware of this factor.

The evaluation of an investment project is also influenced by the possible costs, as mentioned above. The higher the possible costs and losses because of changes in political stability, the more sensitive the companies. Thus industries where the possible losses are largest will be sought. The important factor in this search is probably the capital at stake, or how much money the company has to put into the project. This means that companies in industries where a large amount of capital is needed to make an investment will probably be more sensitive to changes in political stability than other companies. The amount of capital needed and thus the potential losses for an investment can be seen as a function of two things: the economies of scale in the industry, and how capital intensive it is. Those two variables are often correlated. Those variables have partly been taken into consideration already because oligopolies are often built upon them. This phenomenon, however, is perhaps valid on its own because this type of industry is also very inflexible. As a Swedish executive expressed it:

> When an investment is planned, it is to be used for a very long time. I mean, you don't speak of five years, you speak of 15, 20, and 25. And to try to predict the political development for 20 years, I think is totally impossible. But it is obvious that you think twice before you decide to invest in a country which is politically unstable. It has an influence at the moment of decision.*

The quotation above shows that the time you plan for in capital-intensive and large-scale industries is long. This means that companies must be sensitive and react when a country is getting less stable; at the same time it is hard for them to react quickly when a country goes in the other direction, becoming more stable. When this is compared with the situation of a company in an industry where the needed capital for an investment is small, and which is labor intensive, the differences are very clear. A company in the latter industry is very flexible and can therefore react very quickly to changes, and the possible losses are small.

Hypothesis 6:
   Companies in industries where large amounts of capital are needed for an investment will react relatively quickly when a country becomes more unstable, and relatively slowly when a country becomes more stable.

As has been pointed out, companies' evaluation of risks and uncertainties is probably influenced by how dependent the company is on a specific market or product. In many companies it is a policy to diversify geographically or by product in order to decrease the risks for the company as a whole. This has three implications. First, it can be argued that the more diverse a company is, the less sensitive to political stability it is, because one loss does not make a crucial difference for the company. Second, it also can be argued that a diversified company is more sensitive because it does not even have to bother to go into high risk areas. Third, many diversified companies are very decentralized in order to be flexible and react very fast to changes in their environment. Since the argument can be made in both directions, no attempt will be made to formulate a hypothesis.†
   Other economic factors, of course, that are of great importance are business

---

Source: personal interview data, see note, p. 15.
†For a discussion of product diversification see Stopford and Wells (1972, p. 30ff.), of geographical diversification see same (p. 49ff.).

cycles, the economic situation in both the potential host country and in the home country, and the world market price of raw materials. These will be discussed in the empirical analysis.

THE ORGANIZATIONAL OUTPUT PERSPECTIVE

The hypotheses so far have been built upon the notion that the company is rational and makes only one decision. But an investment is not the result of a single decision. It is rather the result of a continuous process involving many people in different roles. As a basis for all activities within the organization there is a consensus on the company's goals and programs. There are also some rules on how activities should be done and how decisions should be made. These rules can be called standard operating procedures or SOPs (Allison 1971, P. 83). If the investment decision is studied from this perspective, the behavior theory approach is stressed. An important reason for this is that the world is very complicated; there is no way for the decision maker to have full information about reality, and there is a cost for getting more information. The result of this is that some rules of thumb (SOPs) must be used and satisfaction instead of maximization becomes a key word. This, in turn, implies that decision makers prefer a satisfying solution with little uncertainty to one that might be maximizing but is uncertain. Risk avoidance might be a rational strategy for the organization as a whole, and thus could have been discussed in the last section. This shows how hard it is to draw a clear border line between the different models.

Simon has pointed out that there are two different types of rationality. The first type is called substantive rationality. According to this type of rationality, a decision maker is rational if he adapts to the situation in such a way that he reaches his goals. For analyzing this type of rationality a theory of situations is needed. The hypothesis presented so far are based upon such theories.

In reality, however, the situation is so complicated, according to Simon, that it is impossible for a decision maker to be substantively rational except in very simple situations. But the decision maker can still be procedurally rational, which means that he can use some rules (SOPs). How successful a decision maker is in attaining his goals depends on how good these rules are. Through feedback and learning, the rules are changed continuously over time.* This argument is valid both at the microlevel for the individual and at the macrolevel for a group of people, that is, an organization.

These rules are important in three different respects, according to Allison

---

*Lecture by Herbert Simon, Harvard University, February 27, 1975.

and Halperin (1972, p. 55): they decide what information is available to the decision makers; they decide which alternatives are considered; and they decide the details when the decision is implemented.

The Decision Process

Aharoni (1966, p. 49ff.) has described the investment decision process using the type of theory discussed above. The process is started by an initiating force. For some reason a person in the company starts to think about a new investment project. This initiating force can have at least three different bases which are qualitatively different. It can be defensive, expansive, or a suggestion from outside the company. If it is defensive, the company is forced to invest if it is not to lose its market. This can be due to competition, as for examples, if another company within the oligopoly has made a similar investment, or if a government has issued new regulations. If the basis for the initiating force is expansive, the company actively tries to enter new markets. The suggestion from outside the company can be from a competitor to form a joint venture or from a government. The latter is often coupled with a "threat" or "offer" of new regulation, which brings us back to the defensive investment.

This description becomes even more logical when complemented by explanations drawn from the organizational behavior model. In the beginning it seems very risky and uncertain even to export to a foreign market. A local agent who knows the country is often needed. But the longer the company has been abroad, and especially in this particular country, the more information and SOPs it has to handle this. The uncertainties become less, and the result in that particular country is satisfying. The company is ready to establish its own marketing subsidiary and later, when it is forced to, its own local manufacturing facilities.

In the other two cases, when the company wants to expand or when it gets a suggestion from outside the company, the situation is much more uncertain, unless the company has already started some local activities and is thus somewhere on the chain defined by the product-cycle theory. The important thing in those cases is probably that the market prospects seem good.

What happens after someone has become interested in a certain investment project depends upon the initiator, the formal organizational structure, and the personalities concerned. Bower also stresses the importance of impetus: someone wants to stand for the project (Bower 1970, p. 57).

The second step in the process is, according to Aharoni, the investigation. This normally has two parts, the so-called armchair investigation, and the field study. (Aharoni 1966, p. 76 ff.). As seen in Chapter 1, a systematic study of the political variables of the investment project is seldom done. The following quotation illustrates very well how the political variables are studied:

When I do an investigation, I do it myself on the basis of sitting down and reading the literature I can find and looking backwards a little.*

That the mass media are of crucial importance for the executive's evaluation of a political situation can be seen in a study made by Zink. In a survey of the same 187 U.S. based companies that we will study, he found that mass media and reports from employees in the country were the two most important sources of information (Zink 1973, p. 38). The same result has been obtained by Keegan (Keegan 1974, p. 414). A study of the sources of information used by executives in export decisions has also been done by Bauer, Dexter, and de Sola Pool. They obtained the following result:

> To the individual businessman, knowledge of the outside world came in a number of ways. It came in part through the printed word, but was surprisingly general and unfocussed. Our respondents read *Time, Business Week, The Wall Street Journal, The New York Times,* and other journals. They read a great deal. They also read trade papers. But, in making a specific business decision, they did not research in public sources. They read what editors chose to provide. Even men with wide foreign business did not read publications from the places where they carried on that business. Knowledge of foreign economic affairs came either from the most general news sources or, more widely, from correspondence and personal experience (Bauer, Dexter, and de Sola Pool 1963, p. 470).

At the same time executives feel they lack pertinent information. This is indicated by Stopford and Wells, who in their survey-study of the 187 U.S. companies found that "general knowledge of local economy, politics and customs" was the most important contribution made by a local joint-venture partner (Stopford and Wells 1972, p. 102–03).

Step number three in the investment decision process is the formal decision to invest. That decision is normally made by the board of directors. The fourth step is the implementation of the formal decision. How each step of the process will look in detail depends upon the routines within the company.

The process can be terminated at any one of several points if the expected result is not forthcoming. But the older a project becomes the higher its chances of survival. This is true for two reasons: First, the uncertainties will decrease during the process as the decision makers get better information and improve routines of collecting it. Aharoni expressed this as follows: "It seems, at least in the developing countries, that the assumed risks are based upon the worst possible likelihood and are therefore reduced by additional information" (Aharoni 1966, p. 99). Second, there is the phenomenon that people who study a project become committed to what they have done by the very fact that they

---

Source: personal interview data, see note, p. 15.

have not rejected it earlier. This argument holds for the company as a whole, too; it becomes committed to projects because of the time and resources it has poured into them.

The first phases of the process, when the uncertainty is great and before anyone is committed, is therefore probably characterized by risk avoidance (Root 1968, pp. 73–79). This means that projects are rejected because they seem very risky and uncertain. But the longer the process continues, the more the decision makers try to keep the project alive, if necessary, by transferring the risk and uncertainty. This can be done, for example, through guarantees, financial measures like local borrowing, or swap loans. In an interview this was described in the following way:

> If there is opposition and there is a possibility that it can gain power, we have to guard ourselves against this. That is why we have a policy to try, at these times, to be as flexible as possible. For several reasons we do not commit too much capital to a country where we . . . are forced to enter.*

During later phases of the process and especially when the investment is made, the company will adapt to the risks in the best possible way. One way of doing this is through inviting local firms and capital into the venture; another is to have as high a proportion of local employees as possible (Hoskins 1970, p. 104).

The investment-decision process is summarized in the figure 2.1 below:

FIGURE 2.1

The Investment-Decision Process

The Decision Process

Initiating force	General investigation	Field investigation	Formal decision	Implementation

---→

                                                                    Time

Risk Strategy

Avoidance		Transfer		Adaptation

Implications For This Study

It thus seems that the crucial factor is whether someone is willing to gamble, to give impetus, to a new project. As seen above, whether this is the case or

---

*Source: personal interview data, see note, p. 15.

not is seldom the result of systematized studies but is rather dependent on intuition and on generalizations obtained through mass media. This has some implications for this study and for its hypotheses.

Since the activities within the firm are regulated by routines, there will be a lag in the change of evaluation rules. If a country is believed to be a good alternative, a relatively high degree of instability is needed to change that opinion (or rule). If, on the other hand, a country is reevaluated and becomes a good alternative, there will probably be a bandwagon effect.

Also, the values and generalizations of a person are in turn dependent upon his home country. The perceptions of what happens in other countries are therefore probably different between companies from different countries. But since it was seen in the Aharoni quote that additional information most often decreases the risk, one can argue that the closer the relationship between home and host country, the less importance the variations in political stability have (See also, Behrman 1974a, pp. 50–51). The following hypothesis can thus be stated.

Hypothesis 7:
  The closer the relationship between the home country and the potential host country, the weaker the correlation between political stability and investment changes.

The close relationship can be based upon geographical proximity, language, ideology, or other special relationships as exemplified by the British Commonwealth. Another type of relationship, although it often correlates with the one just discussed, corresponds to trade and earlier direct investment. The context of political stability changes is also important since there is probably some truth behind the generalizations of countries discussed above. Different taxonomies that can be used to describe the type of country are: tradition of political stability or long-term stability; level of development and size; type of political system;* and region. Some of these have already been mentioned. For example, the level of development is very important to the market size. A taxonomy that will be used very often hereafter is region. Unfortunately enough countries to use other typologies in a meaningful way are not available. When studying those results, however, one should be aware of the high correlation between region and other taxonomies, such as long-term stability.

Another hypothesis of great relevance which cannot be tested with this data is the importance of the experience the company has of business abroad. This

---

*One taxonomy often used in political science is: polyarchic (for example, the West European democracies), centristic (USSR), personalistic (Iran) and traditional (Saudi Arabia).

hypothesis can be deduced from the argument above on the importance of routines and information-gathering systems. With the right data it would have been possible to operationalize the experience by, for example, the time and amounts the company has been investing abroad.

THE BUREAUCRATIC MODEL PERSPECTIVE

The decision process not only proceeds according to rules within the organization; it is also very much dependent upon the power game between different groups within the company. "Players make [company] decisions not by a single rational choice, but by pulling and hauling" (Allison and Halperin 1972, p. 43). The rules and routines discussed in the last chapter can be viewed here as constraints upon the players.

Of decisive importance for the result of the game is the structure of the company and the personalities in that structure. These can be manipulated by the top management. A thesis in normative business administration is that the top management will first decide the company strategy and then find the right structure with the right personalities to implement that strategy. In reality, it is often the other way around; the strategy is decided by the structure. Brook and Remmers found this explanation of investment decisions very important:

> There are . . . the political pressures, the factors operating within the companies' politics, which influence the decision. It is possible to identify certain managerial groups which themselves constitute pressures towards foreign operations, and some which urge opposite policies (Brook and Remmers 1970, p. 25).

In every large organization there has to be a division of functions, and thus different departments for different tasks. There is often a lot of tension between these; each part sees things from a different view and evaluates what is happening in different ways. For example, when a company starts to internationalize through export there is often not a special department for this, but soon a special function and department is needed. This department often becomes the force behind further expansion abroad. Eventually the international department becomes so big that it is better to split it according to product line. Many big companies end up with an organization that is built upon product divisions, geographical divisions, or a combination of these (Stopford and Wells 1972, p. 28; Prahalad 1976, p. 74 ff.). And the bigger this new part is relative to the other parts of the company, the more leverage it will have in deciding future actions of the company.

Parallel to this change in the center of the company are changes in its activities in the field. These changes often follow the sequence export—agent —marketing subsidiary—manufacturing subsidiary, as pointed out earlier.

The same forces earlier observed to be important in the center of the company also work here. When activities have been started in a country, it is possible to find groups both in the center and on the periphery that can speak and argue for investing. It is a self-dynamic process.

Another side of the same coin was mentioned previously when it was observed that the flow of information tends to come from countries where the companies already have activities, which means that those countries have a smaller degree of uncertainty for the company (Keegan 1974, p. 414). The people on the periphery often see the resource allocation function of their central office as their biggest obstacle to expansion, since the sanction of the central office is needed for any large capital investment. This means that the different parts of the periphery have to compete for the scarce resources and are almost forced to tone down all risks and uncertainties and be over optimistic. Many of the executives interviewed were well aware of this.

> It [instability] is of great importance to us, where we in the center perhaps see and are a little bit more anxious than people in the place, in the subsidiary. And it might seem, from their point of view, as if we were generally pessimistic and that we take this as an excuse to moderate their plans for expansion.*

Thus it seems to be a general tendency to down play the importance of the variables that are associated with risk and uncertainty. As seen above, this tendency is probably greater on the periphery of the company than in the center. The president of a subsidiary can very seldom gain anything by discussing political variables; these variables only increase the uncertainty in his plans. This does not mean that political variables are not discussed in reports to the central office; they certainly are, but the problems are minimized.

During the whole investment decision process there is thus a continuous power game going on between different groups and coalitions within the company. To what degree the president of a subsidiary gets his plans and projects accepted depends on his relative influence in the company and how skillful he is at playing the game (Brook and Remmers 1970, p. 39; Stopford and Wells 1972, p. 72ff.). All this makes the process look random and not rational at all. "For all the talk about plans and strategies, the actual decisions arose from chance, almost freakish events" (Brook and Remmers 1970, p. 227).

This section will not be concluded with any hypotheses or modifications of earlier hypotheses. The conclusion is instead that the factors discussed above may provide one explanation if the results expected according to the earlier hypotheses do not materialize in the empirical analysis.

---

*Source: personal interview data, see note, p. 15.

3

OPERATIONALIZATION
OF THE VARIABLES

POLITICAL INSTABILITY EVENTS

When political stability in Chapter 1 was discussed, the conclusion was reached that the influence of "a number of events that can constitute disturbances and increase the political risk" on the investment flows over time should be analyzed. Our task in this section is to choose and operationalize these events.

An operationalization is always a compromise between what is theoretically desirable and what is economically and practically feasible. Since what is wanted is data for a maximum number of countries and types of events for the period since World War II, it is necessary to use one of the existing data collections, or combinations of these, in spite of the weaknesses of these collections (Burgess and Lawton 1972; Drew 1974). The data collection that suits our need best is the *World Handbook of Political and Social Indicators* (*World Handbook* 1971, 1972) which is available on magnetic tape from the Inter-university Consortium for Political Research (ICPR). No other data set contains events data for so many countries for the years from 1948–67. The following variables were chosen to be included in the analysis (for definitions see Appendix B): Renewals of Executive Tenure, Unsuccessful Regular Executive Transfer, Unsuccessful Irregular Power Transfer, Irregular Power Transfer, Regular Executive Transfers, Elections, Protest Demonstrations, Regime-Support Demonstrations, Political Strikes, Riots, Political Assassinations, Armed Attacks, Deaths from Political Violence, Government Sanctions, and Relaxation of Government Restrictions on Political Activity. Many of these events are not disturbances in the normal sense of the word but it was decided to include them because any of them might influence the decision maker's perceptions of risk. Variables that are included in the data set but are not included in the analysis are. Executive Adjustments and External Interventions. The first variable was not included since it did not seem to be an indicator of either change or disturbances. The second variable was not included although it certainly is a disturbance since it refers to the relationship between two countries rather than the domestic situation analyzed in this study.

Data for these variables are given as numbers per year. There is no information on participation, duration, or intensity, so there is no possibility of weighing events together. Every single event is counted as one, and this can of course be severely criticized. The level of aggregation is thus country and year. Preliminary analysis showed that the variable, "number of deaths in political violence," was very skewed and therefore it was decided to use the natural logarithm (ln) of this variable in the subsequent analysis. (The variable called "deaths in political violence" below is thus really "ln deaths.") This means that the effect of the extreme values will be minimized. Doing the analysis it should be remembered that there might be big differences between regions of a country and within one calendar year.

Like most data sets of its kind, *World Handbook* is built on reports in newspapers. This is normally a great problem with this kind of data, but in this case it is known that the decision makers do not make any deeper studies of the countries, which means that what is reported in news media is a good approximation of their information. The huge problem of validity is thus probably smaller than in most other cases when this kind of data is used. *World Handbook* uses the following sources; *L' Annee Politique, Africa Diary, Facts on File, Middle East Journal, Asian Recorder, Associated Press Card File,* and the New York *Times* (index and newspapers) (*World Handbook* 1971, p. 19).

In the first chapter a distinction was made between mass political events and government events. In the analysis these concepts will of course be used, and thus they have to be operationalized here. Government stability is operationally defined as irregular power plus unsuccessful regular executive transfers and unsuccessful irregular power transfers. Mass political stability is defined as riots plus armed attacks and protest demonstrations. The theoretical basis for these two indices was established in Chapter 1. Besides these two indices another index called government transfers will be used in the empirical analysis. This index is operationally defined as irregular power transfers plus regular executive transfers. It was decided to use this index since it was seen in Chapter 1 that government transfers probably have the strongest indirect affect, via the regime under which the companies operate, of any event. All events have been assigned the same weight; no argument could be found for using any other weights.

Operational Definition of Investment

So far the dependent variable has been discussed only as an investment flow, but nothing has been said about how this will be measured. There are two ways to get information about these investment flows; from the nation-state or through the investing companies.

If the nation-state is the source of information, either the outflow from the nation or the inflow into the host country can be studied. Since the primary interest here is in inflows, it is natural to start there.

In the *Balance of Payments Yearbook* of the International Monetary Fund (IMF), the flows of direct foreign investment per year to many countries are shown (Table 11). From this collection we built a data file for the period 1956–70. The time period covered begins at 1956 because IMF changed its accounting system and definitions in 1962, and figures based on the new system are only available from 1956. The time period ends in 1970 because later data were not yet available in any reliable quality. For different countries the degree of specification of the data varies. For some direct investments inflows and outflows are reported, for some just the net figure is given, and for others direct investment is lumped together with other long-term capital movements. Some countries also split up their direct investment into different industrial sectors, for example, oil or mining. We have chosen to use the most specific data for each country, although long-term movement is not used since it is not very relevant to this study. There must be data for at least eight years in sequence for the country to be included in the data set.

Some analysis of this data was done, but both the validity and reliability problems connected with this operationalization are so great that it was decided to use the investing companies as the information source instead.*

---

*The following information-gathering problems were faced:

The price- and exchange-rate. Some data are shown in U.S. dollars, other in the local currency. This is true for one country over time. IMF was followed totally in this respect. When it was necessary to change currency the exchange rates given by IMF were used. Note also that the data is not given in a way that takes into consideration changes in price levels.

Data collection. The data reported is based upon different methods of collection. For some countries it is based upon permissions given, for example, by the central bank. In others they are based upon surveys. Both of these methods have big disadvantages for a study like this, but the most serious is that the same method is not used.

Different definitions of direct foreign investment. An investment can be financed in different ways, through capital transfers, through local or international loans, or through reinvestments of profits. The problem is that different countries include different parts of these funds in their data on foriegn investment, and it is even very hard to know if one country is consistent over time.

The great advantage of using the company as the source of information lies in obtaining information from the organization that is studied. It also makes it possible to put the different companies in groups to test different hypotheses. The difference between this approach and obtaining the information from the nation-state is that in the latter every foreign company that had made an investment in the country should theoretically be included, while in this one can choose which companies to include. The only restriction is that the groups cannot be made too small, because then there will be too much "noise" in the time series.

Data of this type have already been collected by the Harvard Business School Multinational Enterprise Project, and were used here through the courtesy of the project leader, Professor Raymond Vernon. This data collection includes 187 U.S.-based companies and around 200 companies based in the rest of the world. To be included the U.S. companies had to meet two criteria in addition to not being subsidiaries themselves. They had to have been on the *Fortune* list of the "500 Largest U.S. Industrial Corporations" in 1963 or 1964, and they must have held at least a 25 percent equity interest in manufacturing firms in six or more different companies by the end of 1963. When a company met these criteria all firms in which the company had a 5 percent equity interest were included as subsidiaries (Vaupel and Curhan 1969, p. 3ff.). The companies from the rest of the world must have appeared on *Fortune*'s list of the "200 Largest Industrial Corporations" outside the United States in 1970 or had sales as great as the companies included there (Vaupel and Curhan 1973, pp. 2–4). The data collection contains about 12,000 subsidiaries of U.S.-based companies, and 17,000 subsidiaries of companies from the rest of the world.

Reliability of reports. Reliability can be low for several reasons. Some of the more obvious are that many transactions involve bookkeeping within the companies; that there are probably lots of missing data, especially in the developing countries; and that these data have passed through the hands of many people, so that mistakes could easily have been made on the way.

A test of the reliability of this data collection is complicated by the fact that many other authors who have used this data have not noticed that the reporting method often changed between the first year and the final version (Svedberg 1972). Since the data, except for a few cases, is not divided into industries or countries of origin, many of the hypotheses cannot be tested with this operational definition.

The outflows from different countries have been collected by OECD (1967) but then the receiving countries are aggregated. For some countries there are data on outflows of direct investments to specific countries and sometimes even divisions into industries, the United States. But these time series are too short to be useful. This would also create some new problems since the data would be collected far away from the entity under study. It is, for example, easy to show that there are great discrepancies between what is reported as outflows and what is reported as inflows to the same country.

For each subsidiary the year of establishment was given, which means that this operational definition will include newly established subsidiaries, but not reinvestments. Since the decision process is probably very different for new investments and reinvestments this is an advantage. Mergers were excluded since there was no information as to where the parts came from.

Although the project has collected data from the beginning of this century, only the time period since just after World War II (1948) will be treated in this study. Since product lines were given for manufacturing subsidiaries only, these will be included in the analysis. If the subsidiary was incorporated in a country other than the country of its main activities, the latter was chosen as the investment country. From the rest of the world companies referred to, only companies based in Western Europe will be included. Every establishment of a subsidiary abroad by any of these companies in any industry at the three-digit level of the Standard Industrial Classification (SIC) code (1967) counts as one. This means the size of the investment is not taken into consideration, which of course makes the measurement very crude. But, since the investments are aggregated into groups, the same physical investment will be counted as many times as the number of industries in which it manufactures products. Military equipment industries were excluded since they are often established as a result of negotiations between governments.

The result of all this is the following operational definition of foreign direct investment:

An investment is made when any of the companies included in the Multinational Enterprise Project and based in Western Europe or the United States establishes a manufacturing subsidiary abroad by any other means than merger in an industry at the three digit level of the SIC code, except for military equipment industries. Every industry in which the subsidiary manufactures products is counted as one investment.

There are a few things to be noted about this definition. First, the criteria for inclusion are different for investments made by U.S.-based and European-based companies. Second, only positive decisions are included; decisions not to invest are not seen, which might be the most important. Third, there might be a long time between the decision and the actual establishment of a subsidiary, which will constitute a problem for the statistical analysis.

As stated above, a certain number of investments are needed to get useful time series. This means that there will be data only for the countries where there are enough investments made. It also determines how investments will be grouped together. There is thus a limitation on the aggregations which can be done when testing hypotheses concerning industry characteristics. In Chapter 1 it was stated that the independent variable should be changes in investments. These were thus calculated from the aforementioned data set. Consequently the new data file includes only the years 1949–67.

COUNTRIES TO BE INCLUDED IN THIS STUDY

Suppose that for every point in time all countries could be classified by a simple dichotomy as either stable or unstable. Over a period of time one would then be able to distinguish different groups: countries that always are unstable or stable and the ones that are changing groups. The countries that are always perceived as stable are probably not of interest for this study. Therefore, North America, the northern part of Europe, Australia, and New Zealand were excluded (Hibbs 1973, pp. 21–22.) Since this study focuses on changes in investments, countries that have not received any foreign investment cannot be included. Left are the countries that have been unstable during the time period 1948–67 and have received enough investment from abroad.

To know which countries to include, criteria for what constitutes enough investments have to be established. To answer this question a preliminary test was done on both the United States and European data sets. For each year and country all manufacturing subsidiaries established were recorded. A first look at the data showed that the time series are very different for the U.S. and European corporations, and when there was a high correlation between the series, as for Spain, this was due to a growth of investment, giving both series a strong upward trend. It was therefore decided to analyze the United States and Europe separately.

The table below shows the Pearson correlation between the number of subsidiaries established by U.S. and European companies, 1948–67:

Country	r
Mexico	.50
Colombia	.16
Venezuela	.46
Brazil	−.01
Chile	.35
Argentina	.30
France	.43
Spain	.85
Italy	.57

After some preliminary analysis it was then decided that the country must have had 30 or more subsidiaries established by the home country (United States or Europe) to be included. This borderline is of course arbitrary, but below 30 it appears that one single investment has too much influence on the results. There are a few exceptions to this rule:

Rhodesia, Zambia, and Kenya were excluded. Even though they had more than 30 investments from Europe, these investments were lumped together at the year of independence or a similar year. This suggests that these were only legal transfers and not real establishments of subsidiaries that were recorded.

Turkey should perhaps be included for European investments, but was not part of the original data set and therefore was impossible to include.

Peru was excluded because of a programming error, and the cost of going back to correct that mistake was too high.

Pakistan and Nigeria are included in some of the analysis for Europe although they show less than 30 investments. They were included in order to increase the number of countries for the European investments, since the number of countries for Europe is smaller than for the United States. Those two countries were chosen because they had close to 30 investments and because of their geographical and political situations; Pakistan is close to India and Nigeria was experiencing the Biafra conflict.

The result is that the countries in Table 3.1 are included in the analysis.

CLASSIFICATION OF INDUSTRIES

Three hypotheses have been made concerning differences between industries; hypothesis 3 concerned the importance of the degree of oligopoly, hypothesis 5 discussed labor intensity, and hypothesis 6 the amount of capital needed for an investment. In this section the criteria to be used to classify the industries into dichotomies will be presented. More groups cannot be used because of the limited number of investment observations.

Degree of Oligopoly

Oligopoly is a term used to describe the structure of a market where there are only a few sellers. Economic theory teaches that companies in such a market will tend to behave in certain ways.

The most commonly used measure for this market characteristic is the share of the industry's total output produced or sold by the leading companies. This measure is called the n-firm concentration ratio.

This study uses the 4-firm concentration ratio for the U.S. market 1963. This choice can be criticized: First for taking the U.S. market as a base instead of

TABLE 3.1

Countries Included in the Analysis

	Home Countries	
Host Countries	U.S.	Europ
Mexico	X	X
Colombia	X	—
Venezuela	X	—
Brazil	X	X
Chile	X	—
Argentina	—	X
France	X	X
Spain	X	X
Italy	X	X
Nigeria	—	(23)
South Africa	X	X
India	X	X
Pakistan	—	(29)
Philippines	X	—

Note: X indicates more than 30 investments, 1948–67. Figures in parens indicate number of investments when total is below 30.

* Not included in analysis.

Source: Data compiled by the author from the Harvard Business School's Multinational Enterprise project data bank, the *World Handbook* data file, and the International Monetary Fund, *Balance of Payments Yearbook*.

the foreign markets that are studied. Compatible data for the countries analyzed here is not available however, and there is some research indicating that the bias will not be too great. Prayor found that the ranking of industries according to concentration ratios is roughly the same in the developed countries (Prayor 1972, pp. 130–40). But if the absolute level of the concentration ratio is considered as more important, the problem still exists. And nothing is known about the concentration ratios and their importance in developing nations. Second, it is possible to criticize the choice of 1963 as the base year. Some authors have argued that the concentration has grown very much since World War II* Knickerbocker shows, however, that for a sample of U.S. industries there has been a high degree of stability over time. That means the industries have not fluctuated very much compared with each other over time (Knickerbocker 1972, p. 219).

---

*For a thorough discussion of the concentration ratio as a measure of the degree of oligopoly see the introduction to *Concentration Ratios in Manufacturing Industries* (U.S. Congress 1966).

When classifying the three-digit SIC industries into a dichotomy of high and low concentration ratios 60 percent was chosen as the cut-off point. This is an arbitrary choice, since we do not know at which level the oligopolistic behavior really becomes an important part of the companies' behavior. For the classification of the different industries and the data sources, see Appendix C.

Labor Intensity

Measures of labor intensity are most often based upon wages, persons in production, or manhours, all per value added by manufacture. Wages are not a good measure since wages will differ between industries; they probably tend to go down when the labor intensity goes up, which means that the difference between industries will be evened out. The number of persons in production does not take part-time workers into consideration. The best measure, and the one chosen for this study, is probably man-hours in production per value added in manufacture. Again an arbitrary cut-off point had to be selected. One hundred thousand man-hours per million dollar value added was chosen. Appendix C shows the classification of the industries and data sources.

Scale

This can be measured either by total new capital expenditure per establishment per year or average value added per year by manufacture per establishment. The first is really a measure of the average capital needed for one investment in the industry, and the second is a measure of the output per establishment and year in the industry. If we draw a cut-off point for the capital expenditure at $0.15 million and the cut-off point at $3 million (the same as Knickerbocker pp. 134–35, 1972) used for the value added, the classifications are very similar. The only differences are contained in SIC 335 Rolling Non-Ferrous Metal that is included for capital expenditure and in SIC 302 that is included for value added. Both of those industries are included as large scale and thus both cut-off levels are used, whichever is lower. Appendix C shows how the different industries were classified.

The same criticisms raised against the choice of the United States and 1963 as bases for the concentration ratios can of course be raised against the same choices for labor intensity and scale.

COUNTRY PROFILES

Before the main analysis is begun, it might be of help to look at how many and what types of industries the companies have invested in during the period of 1949–67 in the countries studied. This is shown in Table 3.2.

TABLE 3.2

Country Profiles: Investments by U.S. and European Companies, 1948–67

	U.S. Investments				European Investments				
	LS/SS	LLI/HLI	HCR/LCR	No. Inv	LS/SS	LLI/HLI	HCR/LCR	No. Inv	No. Europe/No. U.S.
Mexico	.46	.56	.29	286	.44	1.30	.24	46	.16
Colombia	.41	1.59	.28	106	—[a]	—	—	—	—
Venezuela	.35	.84	.31	138	—	—	—	—	—
Brazil	.35	.81	.20	163	.48	.60	.26	93	.57
Chile	.29	.94	.19	31	—	—	—	—	—
Argentina	.66	1.33	.48	121	.42	.79	.31	68	.56
France	.34	.81	.28	246	.41	.72	.24	181	.74
Spain	.22	1.03	.19	142	.58	.95	.35	109	.77
Italy	.33	.90	.16	222	.43	.77	.33	106	.48
Nigeria	—	—	—	—	.59	1.08	.50	27	—
South Africa[b]	.26	.61	.19	108	.24	.54	.16	229	2.12
India	.30	1.35	.30	61	.46	.46	.27	104	1.70
Pakistan	—	—	—	—	.42	1.40	.13	36	—
Philippines	.40	1.62	.10	55	—	—	—	—	—

Note: LS = large scale; LLI = low labor intensity; SS = small scale; HLI = high labor intensity; HCR = high concentration ration; LCR = low concentration ratio.

[a] Not included in study.

[b] The data for South Africa contain 56 European investments for 1950. Eleven of those investments are in SIC 204 Grain Mill Products and 20 in SIC 205 Bakery Products. This seems much too high; the figures are probably the result of an error in the original data set or just legal transfers.

Source: Data compiled by the author from the Harvard Business School's Multinational Enterprise project data bank, the World Handbook data file, and the International Monetary Fund, Balance of Payments Yearbook.

The absolute numbers show that the largest recipient of U.S. investments measured for this study is Mexico, followed by France and Italy. The European investments have gone to South Africa, within Europe, and to India. But we can see that U.S. companies have invested more abroad than European countries have.

The ratio between the number of European and U.S. investments indicates that difference becomes smaller the farther away we go from the United States. This shows the importance of the geographic and economic distance.

Strangely enough there seem to be relatively more labor-intensive industry investments in the richer and closer countries than in the poorer and more distant nations. This is totally contrary to our expectations. It might be because the manufacturing subsidiaries are established only far away and in marginal markets by large companies using advanced technologies. But on the other hand the same pattern cannot be found for large-scale industries in comparison with small-scale industries, or for high concentration industries in comparison with low-concentration industries. This result could be a function of the fact that the large-scale and high-concentration groups for the average Latin American country contain fewer industries than the low labor-intensive group. If this were the cause then the low labor-intensive industries which are not large scale and high concentration should be closest to the cutoff point of 100. This is, however, not the case. There are certainly industries which are very close, like SIC 287 Agriculture chemicals (98), but there are also industries like SIC 283 Drugs and 284 Soups, the two industries that score lowest on labor intensity.

The pattern of the ratios for European and U.S. companies seems rather similar. The two main differences are the ratios between investments in low and high labor-intensive industries for Mexico and Argentina. It is much higher for Europe in Mexico and much lower in Argentina. This may be caused by the fact that Mexico has a lot of reexport foreign investment from the United States. That tends to be labor intensive, and by the fact that there is a close ethnic link between Argentina and Europe that might be an incentive for European companies to use Argentina as the entry country for Latin America.

II

TEST OF
THE HYPOTHESES

4

ANALYSIS
OF THE RELATIONSHIP

REGRESSION MODELS

The empirical analysis of the relationships between the dependent variables; the changes in investment flows and the independent variables; and the political events will begin in this chapter. In order to find a method to do systematized analysis of a number of countries, Brazil will be first looked at. Brazil is a good example because it has a large market and market growth and both United States and European countries have invested heavily there. There have also been large fluctuations in the political stability since the World War II.

In Figure 4.1, it is possible to see the number of subsidiaries established in Brazil by U.S.- and European-based companies. Below the figure the different time periods and presidents have been marked. There one can see how the American investments really started to grow and overtake the European investments after the World War II.

Before starting the analysis it might be of value to look briefly at Brazil's history. After the World War II, Vargas, who had been dictator since the thirties, was evicted from office. But in the election of 1950 Vargas was again elected. His last presidential period was characterized by weak leadership, inflation, riots, and political strikes. Vargas resigned in August 1954 after he had received an ultimatum to resign from the armed forces. In the next election in 1955 Kubitschek was elected. As a part of a plan to industrialize and develop Brazil, Kubitschek sought to promote a good investment climate to attract foreign investment. But nothing really changed; instead the inflation grew worse at the same time that world prices on coffee depreciated and with that the export income decreased.

In the election of 1960 Quadros, the candidate from the earlier opposition party, was elected. He tried to reform and change Brazil, but in August 1961

FIGURE 4.1

Number of Subsidiaries Established in Brazil, 1948–67

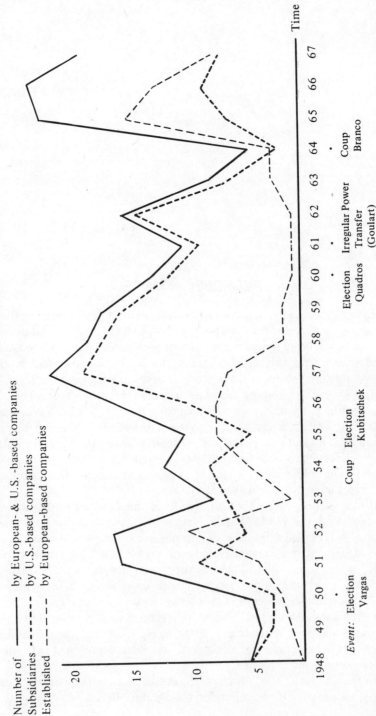

Number of
Subsidiaries
Established

——— by European- & U.S. -based companies

-·-·-·- by U.S.-based companies

– – – by European-based companies

Time

Event: Election Coup Election Coup Election Irregular Power Coup
Vargas Kubitschek Quadros Transfer Branco
(Goulart)

Source: Data compiled by the author from the Harvard Business School's Multinational Enterprise project data bank, the *World Handbook* data file, and the International Monetary Fund, *Balance of Payments Yearbook*.

he resigned—or was forced to resign. Quadros was succeeded by Vice President Goulart. Goulart's presidential powers were, however, very restricted during his first year of government. Inflation became even higher than during Kubitschek's administration, and the situation grew almost chaotic. During the last years of Goulart's presidency the policy toward foreign companies became harder; for example, remittances in excess of 10 percent of invested capital were forbidden, and foreign investment required registration. On March 13, 1964, the oil companies were nationalized. Two weeks later, after a mutiny in the navy, which had the support of Goulart, the military took power. Many thousands of people were arrested. Under the new leader, General Branco, the good investment climate for foreign investment was restored, and inflation was eventually stopped. When Branco was succeeded by General Costa e Silva in 1967, the restrictions on political activities were relaxed (Pollack and Ritter 1975, p. 185; Kantor 1969, p. 649; Weigel 1970).

Comparing this history with the changes in foreign investment, there is obviously a relationship between the two. To test the hypotheses statistically, regression model building using step-wise regression was attempted. This was done first for Brazil and then for the other countries. As dependent variables, changes in the number of subsidiaries established per year by U.S. and European corporations were primarily used but the IMF data was also used. The independent variables were the political event variables from the *World Handbook*. Time lags of 0, 1, and 2 years were used.

The resulting equations were, however, impossible to interpret. This was due to several factors. The large number of independent variables made it impossible to compare equations; in one equation one set of independent variables would be obtained and in the next equation a totally different set of variables would appear. (Appendix D shows some of the resulting equations.)

One might argue though that this is the result of the technique used, that is, step-wise regression. The other way to approach this problem would have been through normal regression. A large number of models would then have to be tested since there is no theoretical base from which such models could have been built. In practice it would have been impossible to do this.

This problem was reinforced by intercorrelations between the event variables. To solve this problem of indeterminancy, the number of independent variables had to be reduced. The standard technique, factor analysis, was tried. The result of the factor analysis seemed quite interesting (see Appendix E). However, these factors were used as independent variables in the regression models, it was realized that these factors were in fact dummy variables for one year during the time period and not a continuously distributed variable. The reason was that the original event-variables were skewed, and the assumptions behind factor analysis were thus broken and this method could not be used.

Another way of reducing the variables is by using additative indices. The analysis was repeated, this time using government stability, mass political stability, and government transfers as independent variables. It was also decided to include "number of deaths in political violence", since this variable often is used as a proxy for mass political stability in political science research (Hudson 1971). Studying the simple Pearson correlation coefficients between these indices and the changes in the investments flows, it was found that the coefficients were low and their direction varied not only between countries but for different time lags and without any pattern. Table 4.1 shows as an example of this the Latin American results for deaths. An attempt was also made absolute investment values with the same result.

TABLE 4.1

Pearson Correlation Between Changes in the Number of Subsidiaries Established and Deaths in Political Violence, Latin America, 1949–67

Country	Investment by U.S. Companies after Political Event (time lag in years)			Investment by European Companies after Political Event (time lag in years)		
	0	1	2	0	1	2
Mexico	−.16	−.11	−.03	.40	−.15	−.28
Colombia	.01	.29	−.10	—*	—	—
Venezuela	−.28	−.17	.18	—	—	—
Brazil	.22	−.33	−.28	−.17	.01	.19
Chile	.31	−.21	.55	—	—	—
Argentina	−.25	.08	−.18	−.14	−.07	0.0

*Not included in study.

Source: Data compiled by the author from the Harvard Business School's Multinational Enterprise project data bank, the *World Handbook* data file, and the International Monetary Fund, *Balance of Payments Yearbook.*

It can be argued that the regression equations should have been controlled for time. This would have been the same as controlling for the increasing expansion of multinational corporations without including these variables. There is no reason to believe that this would have changed the results, however, since much of the earlier discussion was based on Brazil, where the correlation with time is very low (Pearson correlation coefficient for U.S. companies −20 and for European companies .34). Controlling for time is also very dangerous since one might take away the effect of important variables that are correlated with time.

That brings us to the second problem: the interpretation of the time lag. If we get significant equations for different time lags, how should this be interpreted? Should we regard the equations as complementary or as mutually exclusive? They should probably be regarded as complementary since some variables have an immediate effect and others after a certain time lag. But for the same variable we also have the so-called mirror effect: Assume that two variables are identical and have the same four year cycle. If then one of the variables is lagged two years the relationship will still be perfect, but it will be negative. It is impossible to know which time lag is "right."

It is thus hard to make conclusions of any generality with this type of analysis. The problem is too complex, and the data is not good enough to allow the use of this kind of sophisticated statistical methods. Even to describe the relationship between the variables for one single country was difficult (see Appendix D). Perhaps this is due to the assumptions behind regression analysis: The dependent variable is assumed to vary in a corresponding and symmetric way whether the independent variable increases or decreases. In reality, the equations indicated that, especially after government events either a positive or negative change could be obtained in the number of subsidiaries established. This shows that the alternative approach, controlling for time, is not relevant. In fact, regression models are thus not good even for making country-specific conclusions or for describing historical patterns.

This conclusion is supported by some earlier research. Stevens studies the outflow of American direct investment to a number of Latin American countries. He found a negative correlation between this variable and revolutions and government changes for most countries. Looking at the correlation between U.S. investment flow and the number of riots or demonstrations Stevens found a negative relationship for Argentina and Brazil but found no relationship for Mexico and Venezuela. (Stevens 1969, pp. 23–26).

Green has made a study called "Political instability as a Determinant of U.S. Foreign Investment." (Green 1972). As mentioned earlier, most of his study is cross-sectional analysis, but he also studied the annual flow of direct investments to a number of countries.

As his independent variables Green used the data collected by the Feierabends (Feierabends 1966). Their index of political instability is based upon a classification of 30 different types of political events, reported in *Deadline Data on World Affairs* and the *Encyclopaedia Britannica Yearbook*. This index "is based on the theory that a nation's political instability is reflected in the amount of aggressive, politically relevant events occurring within the society" (Green 1972, p. 39). Green used 1, 4, and 8 year averages as bases for the instability index. This index only gives one figure for each country/year, that is, there is no way of differentiating between types of events. Time lags up to three years were used.

For the following nations positive correlations were found: Australia, Canada, France, Italy, Japan, India, Portugal, Spain, United Kingdom, and West Germany. Statistically significant negative correlations were found for the following countries: Argentina, Brazil, Chile, Denmark, the Philippines, and Venezuela. Other countries for which the correlation was negative but not statistically significant were Columbia, Mexico, Peru, South Africa, and Sweden.

Green argues the developed countries have positive relationships while the underdeveloped ones tend to have negative correlations. (Green 1972, p. 73). But it is very hard to draw a borderline between developed and underdeveloped countries, especially since a criterion has to be found that is valid for the whole time period of 1955–68, which is the period Green is studying. How should Portugal be classified, for example, or Japan? One can also ask if a country like Sweden has shown any instability at all on which the companies could have reacted.

Alas, the problem is still there: It is impossible to say if, and in that case when, a political event will be of importance for the investing companies.

CHANGES IN THE INVESTMENT TREND

In the last section explanation of changes in the investment flow using a number of independent variables was attempted. It was assumed that companies react in a symmetric way when a country changes from being politically stable to unstable and when the reverse happens. It was also assumed that a particular independent variable always affects the investment flow after the same time lag. In this section an attempt will be made to loosen those assumptions.

One might ask if all fluctuations in the flow of investment to a country should be explained. Figure 4.2 illustrates this point. It shows cumulatively the number of manufacturing subsidiaries established in Brazil for the period 1948–67. As can be seen in the figure the trend changes only a few times. Or to put it in other words: When the level has been set at a certain level, it stays there until there is a new major change. Instead of explaining all fluctuations in the investment flow, it is thus these trend changes that should be analyzed. Assumptions necessary for regression analysis do not have to be made; instead years of positive trend changes can be compared with years of negative trend changes and years of no trend change. This method also has the big advantage that countries can be grouped together, making testing of the hypotheses and generalizations from the results much easier.

In starting the analysis it has to be decided what should constitute a trend change. Since every country—or dependent variable—is unique, a criterion has to be found that can be used for all the dependent variables. After trying different methods, it was decided to draw the line between trend changes and to make no changes in the following manner:

FIGURE 4.2

U.S. and European Cumulative Investments in Brazil, 1948-67

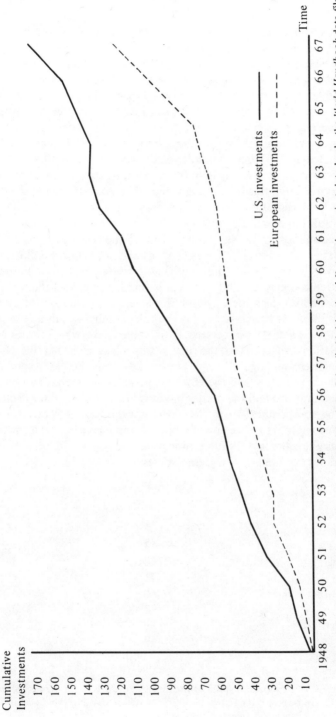

Source: Data compiled by the author from the Harvard Business School's Multinational Enterprise project data bank, the *World Handbook* data file, and the International Monetary Fund, *Balance of Payments Yearbook*.

49

The mean is calculated for the absolute values of the investment changes for the dependent variable. This mean is then multiplied by a constant, so the same value would be high enough to cut off only the years of trend changes from the other years. For the time period 1949–67 the constant was set at 1.5. When this time period was divided into two because of a positive trend (see below) a constant of 1.25 was used for the two resulting time series. This lower value was necessary to neutralize the impact of extreme values. All investment changes greater or the same as the resulting product are considered as positive trend changes; all changes smaller or the same as this product with a negative sign are considered as negative trend changes; the rest constitute no change. Exceptions from this were made if the value was less than 3; then 3 was used as the borderline. Otherwise random factors would have been able to influence the result too much. For European investments in South Africa 10 was used because of the extreme value for 1950 mentioned earlier. For U.S. investments in South Africa 1957–67, 9 was used instead of 11. For the Philippines 1955–67, 5 was used instead of 6. In both cases this was done to minimize the effect of extreme values. One big problem is that it is assumed that a trend change can be defined the same way for the whole time period. This is obviously not true if there has been a large growth in the number of subsidiaries established over the period. As can be seen in the table below which shows the Pearson correlation coefficients for the relationship between the number of established subsidiaries and time (1948–67),* this has been the case especially for the European countries, and therefore the period 1949–67 has been in some cases divided into two and the borderline were then calculated for each subperiod. For the time period 1949–67 the constant was set at 1.5. When this time period was divided into two because of a positive trend (see below) a constant of 1.25 was used for the two resulting time series. This lower value was necessary to neutralize the impact of extreme values.

Country	U.S. companies	European companies
Mexico	.84	.56
Colombia	.62	.68
Venezuela	.53	.52
Brazil	.20	.34
Chile	.71	.49
Argentina	.60	.47
France	.72	.78
Spain	.83	.84
Italy	.69	.83

*Source for table: Data compiled by the author from the Harvard Business School's Multinational Enterprise project data bank, the World Handbook data file, and the International Monetary Fund, Balance of Payments Yearbook.

A small example may clarify this procedure. Imagine we are studying only four years. The flow of investments these years were 6, 1, 4, and 6. This gives changes of –5, +3, +2 and the mean of the absolute values of these changes is 3.330. This multiplied by 1.500 gives 4.995, which is the value that defines what constitutes a trend change. In the example the only trend change thus is –5.

In the above example the time series is very short, the result being that each observation will have too much influence on the definition. This is why it was decided to use the constant of 1.25 when the time series was divided into two parts when there was a strong trend in the time series. If the time series had not been divided when there was a strong (upward) trend, then the last years would have been classified as trend changes, while the first years would have automatically been classified as non-trend years.

There will be three types of years to study: years with a positive trend change, years with a negative trend change, and years with no change of trend. The difference between these types can then be analyzed. This will be done by looking at the mean number of the kind of political events during the different types of years. When looking at only the mean value of events for a certain type of year, one has to be aware that the deviation from this mean can be large; but the number of observations are often too small to make it meaningful to study the standard deviations. Because of this fact, and since by definition the number of years will be very unevenly distributed between the different types of years, most years being no-change years, a more advanced statistical analysis like discriminant analysis that otherwise might have been more efficient cannot be used. When grouping countries together one also has to be careful, for if one country with a low general level on the political variables is grouped together with a country with a high level, the first country will then tend to disappear. With this method the number of observations (years) for each type of year has to be very unevenly distributed; as mentioned above, the result sometimes is dependent upon very few observations. Care must thus be taken when interpreting the results. Time lags will of course be used in the analysis, and what happens years before years of trend change will be observed. Since the investment change variable covers 1949–67 and the political events variables cover 1948–67, a one year time lag can be used without changing the number of observations. But different years will be included for political events: Without time lag 1967 will be included but not 1948 and vice versa when the political variables are logged.

RESULT: LATIN AMERICA

The three Latin American countries for which there are data for both the U.S. and the European companies will be analyzed in this section.

Table 4.2 shows the ratios of the means of the number of events between years of change and no change for the U.S. companies. To the left are the ratios

TABLE 4.2
Ratios between Years of Trend Change and of No Change:
U.S. Investments in Mexico, Brazil, and Argentina

	Time lag = 0		Time lag = 1	
	M^+/M^0	M^-/M^0	M^+/M^0	M^-/M^0
Riots	1.22	0.78	0.77	1.54
Deaths	1.15	1.62	1.72	1.63
Political assassinations	3.25	0/.24	1.47	9.53
Armed attacks	1.03	1.52	2.32	2.81
Elections	0.56	2.21	0.71	1.24
Protest demonstrations	0.69	1.52	2.43	1.60
Regime support demonstrations	3.76	1.20	2.11	3.86
Political strikes	0.92	0.43	0.70	2.77
Renewals of power	2.20	1.40	1.57	6.14
Unsuccessful regular executive transfer	5.50	7.00	0/0.5	2.80
Unsuccessful irregular executive transfer	2.20	5.73	5.58	4.75
Irregular power transfers	0/.20	0/.20	4.71	4.14
Regular executive transfers	1.27	0.66	2.31	2.45
Executions	5.67/0	0/0	0/0	7.29/0
Negative sanctions	1.43	0.92	2.38	1.49
Relaxation of negative sanctions	0.95	0.81	2.61	1.01
Government transfers	0.89	0.46	2.70	2.70
Government instability	1.36	1.58	2.92	3.51
Mass political instability	1.04	1.29	1.75	2.16
Number of years of change/ Number of years of no change	9/41	7/41	9/41	7/41

Note: M^+ = Mean number of [events] during years of positive change; M^- = Mean number of [events] during years of negative change; M^0 = Mean number of [events] during years of no change. 0/XX signifies that there were no events of that type during the years of change, XX being the mean number of that event during the years of no change; XX/0 signifies that there were no events of that type during the years of no change, XX being the mean number of that event during the years of change.

Source: Data compiled by the author from the Harvard Business School's Multinational Enterprise project data bank, the *World Handbook* data file, and the International Monetary Fund, *Balance of Payments Yearbook.*

for the same year and to the right are the ratios for what happened the year before (one year time lag). Ratios between years of change and years of no change are used since only the relative frequency of the events among the different types of years is of interest. A ratio of 2 for positive-trend change-years means, for example, that there are twice as many of those events in the average year of positive trend change as in the average year of no change.

When there is no difference between the types of years, the ratio will be 1, and when the mean frequency of an event is lower years of change than years of no change (positive or negative) then the ratio will vary between 1 and 0.

Looking first on the political events the same year as the trend change, there seems to be little difference between years of positive trend change and years of no change.

On the other hand, years with negative changes seem to be years with a generally high level of violence and disturbances. Deaths, armed attacks, government instability, and mass instability are all high. The right side of the table shows a very clear pattern the year before the trend changes. Almost every type of event is higher during years before both positive and negative trend changes. For those countries the companies very clearly react to the political events in the countries.

The main difference between positive and negative changes is that the level of disturbances is even higher in years before negative changes, that is, the ratios are in general somewhat higher for the latter type of trend changes. That the investment flow often increases during years after political disturbances is probably due to the fact that these disturbances constitute, cause, or coincide with policy changes toward the foreign companies. This result really shows the importance of the government events.

This result is stable if the other Latin American countries are included too: Colombia, Venezuela, and Chile.

In Table 4.3 the same numbers for the European investments in Mexico, Brazil, and Argentina can be seen. The European investments increase in these countries when the political protest is low the year before. The level of political deaths, however, is higher the same year. All the ratios for Europe are much closer to 1 than for the United States; care must therefore be made when forming conclusions. The result is similar for Europe and the United States concerning government transfers; in both cases this variable has a high frequency in years before positive changes.

Turning to negative trend changes one finds that for the current year only government transfers, and especially irregular power transfers, are higher than the other years. In the year before the change most ratios are actually lower, meaning that the mean number of events is low the year before the years of negative change; then we have an increase in the political instability to the year of change. This increase causes negative change. But there are two alternative, more technical, explanations of why the ratios are lower for the years before negative trend changes. The first concerns the interdependence in the measurement of the events data. Consider a country that has an even level of political stability except for one year when all the events have a high frequency and when there is a negative trend change. In the data the ratio for the year of negative change will be high, but for the year before the year of negative change, the ratio will be lower, since in the calculation of the mean for the

TABLE 4.3

Ratios between Years of Trend Change and of No Change: European Investments in Mexico, Brazil, and Argentina

	Time lag = 0		Time lag = 1	
	M^+/M^0	M^-/M^0	M^+/M^0	M^-/M^0
Riots	0.82	1.06	1.19	0.56
Deaths	1.47	1.07	1.16	1.02
Political assassinations	0.30	0/.37	0/.40	0.50
Armed attacks	0.66	0.01	0.49	0.36
Elections	0.01	0.95	0.67	1.05
Protest demonstrations	0.61	1.09	0.53	0.38
Regime support demonstrations	0/1.12	0.18	0.31	1.12
Political strikes	1.30	0.97	0.83	0.55
Renewals of power	1.83	0/.12	0/.16	0/.16
Unsuccessful executive transfer	0/.07	0/.07	0/.07	0/.07
Unsuccessful irregular executive transfer	0/.33	0.61	0.37	0.67
Irregular power transfers	0.92	3.33	1.57	0/.14
Regular executive transfers	0.70	0.85	2.11	1.00
Executions	0/1.19	0/1.19	0/1.19	0/1.19
Negative sanctions	0.55	0.56	0.62	0.37
Relaxation of negative sanctions	0.42	4.47	0.74	0.24
Government transfers	0.76	1.38	1.96	0/.51
Government instability	0.61	0.92	1.06	0.19
Mass political instability	0.70	1.05	0.69	0.41
Number of years of change/ Number of years of no change	9/43	5/43	9/43	5/43

Note: M^+ = Mean number of [events] during years of positive change; M^- = Mean number of [events] during years of negative change; M^0 = Mean number of [events] during years of no change. 0/XX signifies that there were no events of that type during the years of change, XX being the mean number of that event during the years of no change; XX/0 signifies that there were no events of that type during the years of no change, XX being the mean number of that event during the years of change.

Source: Data compiled by the author from the Harvard Business School's Multinational Enterprise project data bank, the *World Handbook* data file, and the International Monetary Fund, *Balance of Payments Yearbook.*

no-change years with one year time lag the year of negative change will be included, while the year before the trend change will comprise only one year with the normal level of political stability. The second explanation is that often a strong positive trend change is followed by a reaction: the investment flow goes back to normal. This, however, will sometimes be recorded as a negative trend change in the time series. The data support this latter explanation to some extend but not more for Europe than for the United States.

Comparing the U.S. and European investments it can be said that the U.S. companies increase their investments in these countries in years following years with a high level of political violence. European countries increase their investments substantially only when both the year before and the current year have a low level of mass political events. For both U.S. and European companies, government transfer seems to be important, independent of whether or not this happens through regular transfer or coups. The U.S. companies decrease their investments in years of, and especially years following, a high frequency of all political events. For the European companies the government transfers the same year seem to be important for decreases. The ratios are overall much higher for the U.S. companies, implying that they have reacted more to the political events; that is, the percent of the total number of events that happens right before or during trend changes is greater for U.S. companies than for European.

The hypotheses seem to be supported by the data so far. The companies react to political events or to other changes in their environment that are highly correlated with these political events. For both U.S. and European companies government events seem to be of overriding importance. Mass political instability seems to be of little importance to the European companies, but the U.S. companies seem to react negatively to this.

Further, looking at the time lags, it seems as if the companies react negatively the same year but are slower to react positively. This can be interpreted as follows: the companies react negatively to all mass political violence, but if this violence is accompanied by a government change that is perceived as positive by the companies, for example in the form of general economic policy or policy towards foreign investments, then the companies will increase their investments again. The different in time lag becomes even more interesting when compared with Hudson's results. He showed that in Latin America government transfers tend to occur in the year of maximum crisis (number dead in political violence). This shows that the result is not only due to a correlation between transfers and mass political violence with one year time lag. (Hudson, 1971, p. 273).

FRANCE, SPAIN, AND ITALY

These countries were analyzed together although there are big differences between them. Spain has had the same government during the whole period and this government can be characterized as repressive. Italy on the other hand has had a large number of governments and riots and demonstrations are part of the political life there.

The results for these countries are shown in Tables 4.4 and 4.5. As pointed out earlier there has also been a strong trend of increasing investments in these countries. Therefore two time periods were used when defining the trend

TABLE 4.4

Ratios between Years of Trend Change and of No Change:
U.S. Investments in France, Spain, and Italy

	Time lag = 0		Time lag = 1	
	M^+/M^0	M^-/M^0	M^+/M^0	M^-/M^0
Riots	0.90	1.44	1.24	0.31
Deaths	0.50	1.45	1.10	0.25
Political assassinations	0/.08	0/.08	0/.08	0/.08
Armed attacks	0.83	3.35	0.63	0.96
Elections	1.79	3.57	1.86	0.61
Protest demonstrations	1.13	1.16	1.90	1.57
Regime support demonstrations	2.45	2.47	1.88	1.07
Political strikes	0.77	1.05	0.93	0.21
Renewals of power	1.02	0.73	1.26	0.37
Unsuccessful executive transfer	0.44	0.58	1.00	0/1.75
Unsuccessful irregular executive transfer	0/.03	0/.03	0/0	0.11/0
Irregular power transfers	0.08/0	0/0	0.80/0	0/0
Regular executive transfers	0.91	0.52	1.37	0.16
Executions	0.49	0.33	0/.42	4.50
Negative sanctions	0.83	1.56	1.05	1.09
Relaxation of negative sanctions	0.78	1.39	1.14	2.19
Government transfers	0.98	0.54	1.69	0.17
Government instability	0.89	0.67	1.27	0.28
Mass political instability	1.22	2.37	1.02	0.57
Number of years of change/ Number of years of no change	12/36	9/36	12/36	9/36

Note: M^+ = Mean number of [events] during years of positive change; M^- = Mean number of [events] during years of negative change; M^0 = Mean number of [events] during years of no change. 0/XX signifies that there were no events of that type during the years of change, XX being the mean number of that event during the years of no change; XX/0 signifies that there were no events of that type during the years of no change, XX being the mean number of that event during the years of change.

Source: Data compiled by the author from the Harvard Business School's Multinational Enterprise project data bank, the *World Handbook* data file, and the International Monetary Fund, *Balance of Payments Yearbook.*

changes, as mentioned above. After the data was looked at, the border between the two periods was set at 1958–59. The results from these two periods were then weighed together in order to get the result for the whole period 1949–67 as shown in the tables.

Table 4.4 shows that in years of positive changes in American investments the frequency of almost all types of events except protest demonstrations is

TABLE 4.5

Ratios between Years of Trend Change and of No Change: European Investments in France, Spain, and Italy

	Time lag = 0		Time lag = 1	
	M^+/M^0	M^-/M^0	M^+/M^0	M^-/M^0
Riots	1.15	1.76	0.34	0.96
Deaths	0.39	0.82	0.33	1.05
Political assassinations	1.80	0/.05	0/.08	0/.08
Armed attacks	0.43	1.69	0.37	0.30
Elections	0.18	1.18	0.37	0.41
Protest demonstrations	2.04	3.53	0.86	2.59
Regime support demonstrations	0.79	0.57	1.02	0.58
Political strikes	0.99	1.63	0.32	0.43
Renewals of power	0.39	1.72	0.47	0.48
Unsuccessful executive transfer	0.49	0.36	1.25	0.55
Unsuccessful irregular executive transfer	0/0	0.20/0	0/.02	0/.02
Irregular power transfers	0/.03	0/.03	0/.03	0/.03
Regular executive transfers	0.41	0.58	0.49	0.27
Executions	0.22	4.39	0.42	1.07
Negative sanctions	1.16	1.31	0.77	1.30
Relaxation of negative sanctions	1.23	1.68	0.75	0.66
Government transfers	0.39	0.56	0.47	0.25
Government instability	0.41	1.31	0.61	0.47
Mass political instability	0.90	2.04	0.44	0.87
Number of years of change/ Number of years of no change	11/41	5/41	11/41	5/41

Note: M^+ = Mean number of [events] during years of positive change; M^- = Mean number of [events] during years of negative change; M^0 = Mean number of [events] during years of no change. 0/XX signifies that there were no events of that type during the years of change, XX being the mean number of that event during the years of no change; XX/0 signifies that there were no events of that type during the years of no change, XX being the mean number of that event during the years of change.

Source: Data compiled by the author from the Harvard Business School's Multinational Enterprise project data bank, the *World Handbook* data file, and the International Monetary Fund, *Balance of Payments Yearbook.*

lower than during years of no change. For the year before the change the difference is very small. But there is one interesting thing to note: During this year the government transfers are higher than the other years.

For the years of negative trend change, most of the mass political violence variables are all high; riots, deaths, and armed attacks are very high. The frequency of government events on the other hand is low. For the earlier year almost all the variables have low values. This shows the importance of mass political stability to the companies' investment behavior and how quickly it reacts when the instability increases.

The European companies increase their rate of establishing subsidiaries in these three countries when both the current year and the year before have been very stable (Table 4.5). The negative changes in European investments happen in years when the mass political violence is very high and government renewal of power is high. Government transfers have no importance to European investments. Elections are most common during years of negative changes and least common during years of positive changes both for the U.S. and European investments. This probably shows the uncertainty that managers experience before an election.

In comparing the European and American investments in France, Spain, and Italy, it can be seen that for positive trend changes a general stability seems to be of vital importance. The U.S. companies react positively to government transfers too. For the negative changes the level of mass political violence seems to be the important thing. The years of negative changes are character-ized by a high frequency of those variables. Government changes are of little importance.

As for the investment pattern for Latin America, the negative reaction for Europe is immediate, while the positive trend change is not dependent upon a specific event. In fact the phenomenon that the frequency of many events is lower the year before negative changes can again be seen. The pattern seems to be similar in many respects for the Latin American and European countries. The main difference between the two regions seems to be the fact that in Latin America a high level of mass political violence is often accompanied with government events, or vice versa (Hudson 1971, p. 268). If this new govern-ment pursues a policy that the companies believe is good for them, the invest-ments increase.

It is very hard to find any substantial differences between the behavior of the American companies and the European ones. But the difference in the political culture in Latin America and Europe can be seen by looking at the variables. Government transfers in Latin America are mainly irregular power transfers, while in Europe they are regular executive transfers. The importance of elections in Europe has already been pointed out; that event, however, seems to have no relevance in Latin America.

OTHER COUNTRIES

As pointed out earlier, countries can only be grouped together with roughly the same level of disturbances. Since the rest of the countries for which there is data are very disparate, they have to be analyzed separately. The only exception is the European investments in India and Pakistan. This means that the number of observations will be very small; for many countries there is only one negative change and one positive change. Thus, when one looks at this data and tries to interpret what has happened, one has to be very careful. The results for all these countries plus the countries already analyzed are summarized in Table 4.5. The conclusions drawn from Latin America and Europe seem to be supported by the data for these countries.

In India the U.S. investments increase immediately after government transfers. For decreases government events are of decisive importance, while the level of mass instability is lower in both years. The European investments in both India and Pakistan (there is no major difference between the two) show the importance of government events; for the negative changes these are accompanied by mass violence. Contrary to what was found in Latin America, the government events come first followed by mass violence and a change in investment.

The data for the Philippines includes only 1956–67 since there is very little investment before 1956. That fact might be a result of the very high level of disturbances in the early 1950s when the Philippines experienced what might be called a civil war: the Huk rebellion.

The U.S. companies seem to react with a one year time lag in the Philippines. The investments increase one year after a high level of government transfer and decrease one year after a high level of mass political instability (for example, armed attacks).

In Nigeria the European investments increase when the level of all types of disturbances are high and have been high; it decreases during a year of government instability. The result for Nigeria is influenced by the Biafra conflict which shows up in the data 1966 and 1967. If those two years are excluded, the level of mass political violence is not much lower during years of negative change than other years. One of the positive changes is 1967, which means that the high values for positive change come from this year. The conflict obviously did not stop the companies from investing in Nigeria.

When these results are compared with the earlier findings, the importance of government transfer both for positive and negative trend changes and for U.S. and European companies can again be seen. Negative changes tend to occur the same year as the disturbances. The only clear exception is the Philippines.

To draw any conclusions about the differences between the European and American companies is very hard, if not impossible, since there is no data for the same countries.

Finally a very particular country will be looked at: South Africa. It is totally different from all other countries, since investment there has become a moral question where public opinion in the companies' home countries to a large extent influences the investment decision. This has not, however, stopped the countries from investing in South Africa.

Looking at the European investments first, we see the normal pattern for the negative changes: mass political violence is higher the year before, and government changes are high the years of the changes. But looking at the positive changes, we see that these are accompanied by very high levels of violence but very few government events. This is contrary to our earlier results.

The results for the American companies' investments in South Africa are also strange. For the negative changes, all events, except for the number of deaths the year before, are lower than in other years. For positive changes, however, government events are important. These results may be because South African policy changed around 1960, the year of high increases of investments and of mass political violence. This policy change probably had a stronger effect than the outburst of violence that the government seemed able to handle; in 1960, the year of the Sharpville massacre, the acts of negative sanctions increased tremendously.

CONCLUSIONS

It is now time to summarize the findings from this chapter. Regression models were first tried in analyzing the relationship between the variables. This was not a viable method, however, because of the many assumptions behind regression analysis. Instead it was concluded that what is really of interest is major changes in the trend of the number of manufacturing subsidiaries established. The main bulk of the chapter was then devoted to an analysis of what characterizes years of and before the positive and negative trend changes respectively (see Table 4.6).

When summarizing the result of this analysis, the hypotheses from Part I will be used, and it will be seen how these hypotheses stand for the evidence presented. It was found that the level of either or both government events and mass political events are higher the year of or before negative trend changes. That is, the companies seem to decrease their investments in response to these events. For positive trend changes the results are more complicated but as a general observation one can say that hypothesis 1, "The investments in a country decrease when a country is unstable and increase when it is stable," seems to be confirmed. But as mentioned above and as expected this generalization has to be extended and developed.

The reaction seems to be asymmetrical. A high level of mass political violence makes the companies decrease their investment relatively fast, but a low level of political disturbances is not enough for them to increase their investment. Instead there often has to be an impulse in the form of government transfer. If this in turn means that a change in policy is necessary is not known, but it can be guessed that it has to be perceived by the companies as a change in the general economic policy in the country. This will be discussed later. Government events and especially transfers that seem to be of vital importance both for positive and negative changes are, however, often preceded or accompanied by mass political disturbances. The years before positive trend changes are often violent.

The data supports hypothesis 2, stated previously as follows: "Government disturbances will be followed either by an increase or a decrease in investment, in both cases of a larger size than after mass political events." It must be pointed out, though, that we have not really made an analysis of the causal relationship. It can only be said that both increases and decreases occur together with government disturbances.

The differences between types of industries have not yet been studied, so hypotheses 3, 5, and 6 cannot be answered. Hypothesis 4 describes the importance of markets: "The larger the market and/or market growth ... the weaker the relationship." There was also a general discussion of the possible differences between different types of countries in Part I.

What has been found? It should be noted that in this first analysis, countries have only been divided by regional group and not by market size. Nothing can be said yet about hypothesis 4. But it is possible to compare European and Latin American countries and sometimes the other analyzed countries can be taken into the discussion too.

The main difference between the European countries and the others seems to be that in Europe the negative changes occur together with mass political instability only, while in the other countries government events seem to be relatively more important. Paradoxically, this means that mass political instability as a phenomenon of its own is of more importance in Europe than elsewhere. Other countries also have mass political instability preceding or dúing the years of change, but this violence is caused by, or causes, government events that sometimes make the companies decrease, sometimes increase, their investments, depending upon how the new government is perceived.

In Europe a general stability is enough for the investments to increase. This difference is probably because under normal conditions political variables are of little importance in Europe, but when the disturbance level increases above a certain threshold, it is perceived as a threat. In Latin America, on the other hand, political violence is a normal part of the political life; managers are used to living with it and do not care too much when it goes up and down.

Hypothesis 7 discusses the importance of the companies' home countries: "The closer the relationship between the home-country and the potential host country, between political stability and investment changes the weaker the correlation between political stability and investment changes."

Looking at the similarities and dissimilarities between the American and European companies in the three Latin American countries and in the three

TABLE 4.6

Ratios between Years of Trend Change and of No Change: Summary Table

Home Country	Trend Change	Time Lag	Government Transfers	Government Instability	Mass Political Instability	Deaths
Mexico, Brazil, Argentina						
United States	positive	0	.89	1.36	1.04	1.15
	positive	1	2.70	2.92	1.75	1.72
	negative	0	.46	1.58	1.29	1.62
	negative	1	2.70	3.51	2.16	1.63
Europe	positive	0	.76	.61	.70	1.47
	positive	1	1.96	1.06	.69	1.16
	negative	0	1.38	.92	1.05	1.07
	negative	1	0/.51	.19	.41	1.02
France, Spain, Italy						
United States	positive	0	.98	.89	1.22	.50
	positive	1	1.69	1.27	1.02	1.10
	negative	0	.54	.67	2.37	1.45
	negative	1	.17	.28	.57	.25
Europe	positive	0	.39	.41	.90	.39
	positive	1	.47	.61	.44	.33
	negative	0	.56	1.31	2.04	.82
	negative	1	.25	.47	.87	1.05
South Africa						
United States	positive	0	.77	1.37	.27	.92
	positive	1	0/.43	0/1.50	.75	1.69
	negative	0	0/.43	.41	.30	.88
	negative	1	0/.43	.33	.51	1.38

Europe	positive	0	0/.29	.44	5.87	1.64
		1	0/.43	0/1.50	1.79	1.89
	negative	0	3.44	1.75	.77	.69
		1	0/.43	.22	4.23	1.23
India						
United States	positive	0	4.17	1.32	.08	.92
		1	0/.35	0/1.47	1.21	1.10
	negative	0	8.33	1.97	.19	.78
		1	0/.35	.68	.15	.63
India-Pakistan						
Europe	positive	0	2.32	1.20	.66	.57
		1	3.00	1.34	.38	.52
	negative	0	1.16	1.60	6.22	.74
		1	6.00	2.87	1.43	1.06
Philippines (1956–67)						
United States	positive	0	0/.44	0/.67	.20	.64
		1	3.00	1.49	.32	.82
	negative	0	0/.44	.75	.28	.89
		1	0/.33	0/.67	1.08	1.24
Nigeria						
Europe	positive	0	2.00	2.00	5.23	2.54
		1	5.26	4.54	3.72	2.05
	negative	0	8/.25	2.00	.09	0/2.33
		1	0/.19	0/.44	.12	0/2.03

Source: Data compiled by the author from the Harvard Business School's Multinational Enterprise project data bank, the *World Handbook* data file, and the International Monetary Fund, *Balance of Payments Yearbook.*

European countries, it was possible to detect some weak evidence for this. It seems as if the relationship is stronger for the Americans in Latin America and for the Europeans in Europe.

Before ending this chapter it should be mentioned what has been shown this far. First, a relationship between political events and changes in investments that seems to support the hypotheses generated in Part I has been established. But it has not been shown that the changes in investment really are caused by political events. This is very hard to do in any social science research, but the least one has to do is to include other potentially important variables in the analysis. This obviously has to be done before any firm conclusions can be drawn. One variable that has been shown indirectly to be of importance is government policy or perceived policy.

Second, in this chapter it has been shown that the level of disturbances often is correlated with changes in investments. But at the same time it has also been found that the level of disturbances can be low or high without any change in the investment trend. It has not been shown under which conditions the political events are of importance.

Third, and last, changes or breaking points in the trend have been discussed without mentioning the slope of that trend. This is obviously of great importance and might also be a source of bias for the results. Imagine, for example, a country where the frequency of political disturbances increases and stays high for a number of years and then goes down again. If the hypotheses are right, this means that the investment flow will first go down when the frequency goes up, and up when the country becomes stable again. This will be recorded in the data as a negative trend change year, a number of no-change years, and one positive change. The respective change years will thus be compared with the average of both years of high and low stability. This shows that the analysis is based on the assumption that the normal situation is "stable" and that unstable periods are of relatively short duration. In view of the data, this assumption seems not as simplifying as one might first think. It is very seldom that the level of violence stays high for a number of years. But in the cases when a country experiences a prolonged crisis with a high frequency of political disturbances, this assumption does not hold. One may argue that changes in the frequencies of the political events should have been used instead, but then the absolute level of political stability would not have been taken into the analysis.

5

**ADDITIONAL
EVIDENCE**

POLITICAL EVENTS—A SUFFICIENT CONDITION FOR CHANGE?

So far it has been shown that there is a relationship between political events in a country and the establishment of manufacturing subsidiaries in that country by large multinational corporations. In the social sciences it is always hard if not impossible to establish causal relationship. A found correlation can be caused by a third variable that influences both the studied variables, or the causal relationship might go through an intermediate variable; in both these cases a change in the independent variable is neither sufficient nor necessary for a change in the dependent variable.

The implication is, first, that it is necessary to study other potentially relevant variables that might influence both the variables, such as the economic situation in the country; secondly, that possible intermediate variables must be studied. The clear example of this, mentioned earlier, is policy. Thirdly, one must specifically look at whether disturbances are a sufficient condition. The latter will be covered first.

When relationships between the political events and investments flows were studied above, investment flows were analyzed first and then the political events associated with the trend changes. The conclusion was that even if political events are not a necessary condition for trend changes, most trend changes are associated with high or low frequencies of the different political events.

This type of conclusion is very common in the social sciences because the relationships studied are so complex and seldom deterministic, while statistical techniques are also stochastic rather than deterministic. As a complement to the earlier analysis it is necessary therefore to look also at the independent variable and then observe the effect on the dependent variable. This will help to answer the question whether political disturbances are a sufficient condition for trend changes. To do this analysis the years of highest violence (determined by the number of political deaths) for each country during the second half of the period 1948–67 were taken to see if these were followed by a negative change for U.S. investments.

The result is shown in Table 5.1. A decrease in investments is often associated with a high level of instability, but almost as often there is a very weak reaction or no reaction at all. The relationship between years of high disturbances and the years of trend changes (not shown in the table) is the same.

TABLE 5.1
Investments in Years of Maximum Violence

Country	Years of High Deaths[a]	Investments	
		Same Year	Year After
France	1962	decrease	decrease
	1958	increase	increase
Spain	1960	weak increase	no change
Italy	1960	decrease	increase
Mexico	1961	increase	decrease
	1967	decrease	—[c]
Colombia	1955	weak decrease	increase
	1956	increase	decrease
	1964	decrease	increase
Venezuela	1958	no change	increase
	1962	decrease	weak increase
Brazil	1966	increase	decrease
	1962	increase	decrease
Chile	1957	no change	no change
Argentina	1955[b]	decrease	increase
	1962	increase	decrease
South Africa	1959	decrease	increase
	1957	decrease	increase
Philippines	1959	weak increase	decrease
	1967	weak increase	—
India	1958	increase	weak decrease
	1967	weak decrease	—

[a] The largest increase/decrease first for a given country.

[b] 1956 also has a relatively high level of violence.

[c] No data exists for these entries.

Source: Data compiled by the author from the Harvard Business School's Multinational Enterprise project data bank, the *World Handbook* data file, and the International Monetary Fund, *Balance of Payments Yearbook.*

The high level of instability is often associated with the changes in the investment trend, but they also often occur during periods of only minor changes that started with major negative changes or sometimes even positive trend changes.

Obviously a high level of violence is not a sufficient condition for a decrease in the investment flow. In other words, it was shown that political disturbances are sometimes very important, but it is not known how they interact with other variables. In the figure below a few of the possible relationships between the variables have been drawn.

RELATIONSHIPS BETWEEN ECONOMIC INDICATORS AND INVESTMENT FLOW

To study the importance of the economic situation within the host country to the foreign investors, the correlation between some economic indicators and the number of subsidiaries established per year was calculated. The indicators used were Gross Domestic Product (GDP), change in GDP, Gross Domestic Capital Formation, and Exports and Inflation (United Nations 1948–67).

There were many problems encountered, since indicators at fixed price were desired. For GDP and its changes there were also problems because for some countries the GDP at factor price was given, for others GDP at market price, and for Chile only the Net Domestic Product. Of course there are also the other problems common to this type of data and discussed in Chapter 3. Because of these problems there were restrictions and only data for shorter time periods for most countries could be obtained. Thus the number of observations is relatively few.

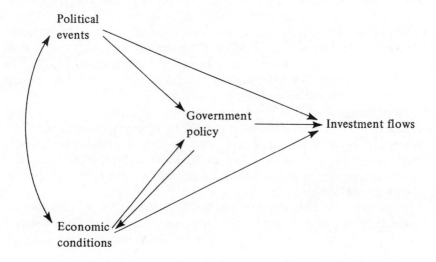

The result showed that there was little correlation between these indicators and the flow of investments. In a few cases, such as Spain and Mexico, the coefficients are high, but that is only a function of both variables being highly correlated with time (Table 5.2).

It is rather surprising that the correlations are not higher, because even if the direct importance of the economic situation is minor, there should be an indirect relationship via the government and its policy, influencing both the economic situation in the country and foreign direct investments. This lack of correlation might be due to the fact that, in less developed countries especially, the economic situation is decided by external factors like world prices on raw materials.

There can also be a fit between the trend changes of the investments and major changes in the economic situation without this relationship showing in the correlation coefficients. Analysis of the data seems, at least to some extent, to support this.

A similar result has been obtained by Weigel (Weigel 1970) who tried to explain fluctuations in U.S. investment flow to Brazil with the rate of return on foreign investments in Brazil adjusted for inflation, exchange rate changes, and restrictions on capital repatriations. He was not able to get a significant result unless he added a dummy variable to the model for political stability 1960–64.

IMPORTANCE OF THE REGIME

In Chapter 1 the regime was defined as "the rules under which the economy, including foreign companies, works in the country. On different levels of abstraction these rules consist of the ideology of the government, the generalized policy, and how this policy is applied."

The lower levels of policy are of course to a large extent defined by the higher policies; the higher the level of policy, the more seldom will it change, given the same government. The ideology of the government will probably stay the same during its whole tenure, while the economic policy and policy towards foreign investments can be changed during the tenure.

As argued in Part I the changes in ideology will thus coincide to a large extent with government transfers, important to the investing companies. Government transfers are so important probably because of the accompanying change in political color of the government rather than the transfer per se. This is supported by the observation that not all transfers cause major changes in the investment flow.

A similar conclusion has been reached by Rosen (1974, p. 118) who explained the changes in foreign investment by an "Open Door Theory," stating that "General rightward and leftward political changes in other countries

TABLE 5.2

Pearson Correlation between Some Economic Indicators and the Number of Subsidiaries Established

		GDP[a]	GDCF[b]	Export	Inflation	Inflation Rate Change
Mexico	US[c]	.55	—[e]	—	-.37	-.14
	EU[d]	.54	—	—	.20	.16
Colombia	US	.32	.06	.40	.24	.19
Venezuela	US	.02	-.43	—	—	-.14
Brazil	US	-.41	-.07	-.19	.58	.64
	EU	.10	.22	.59	-.45	-.31
Chile	US	.28	.10	.40	-.19	-.52
Argentina	US	.16	.48	.03	.16	-.13
	EU	.21	.13	-.21	.12	.26
France	US	-.81	-.44	-.75	—	.35
	EU	.68	.40	.69	—	.30
Spain	US	.82	.79	.80	—	.29
	EU	.92	.89	.91	—	.27
Italy	US	.08	.37	-.02	—	-.20
	EU	.76	.65	.78	—	-.13

[a] Gross Domestic Product.
[b] Gross Domestic Capital Formation.
[c] By U.S. firms.
[d] By European firms.
[e] Data not available.

Source: Data compiled by the author from the Harvard Business School's Multinational Enterprise project data bank, the *World Handbook* data file, and the International Monetary Fund, *Balance of Payments Yearbook*.

specifically affect the degree to which the door is open de jure and de facto to U.S. private trade and investments." Studying Brazil, Indonesia, Chile, Greece, and Peru, countries that have experienced radical changes in the color of the government in power, Rosen (1974, p. 135) found that to be true for government transfers in all except Greece.

With regard to economic policy, it was seen in the last section that there is little correlation between the outcome of that policy, the economic situation, and the investment flows. Evaluating this result one must also consider, however, that many countries included in this analysis are extremely sensitive to external factors, that is, the government can do very little to influence the economic situation of the country, at least in the short run.

Policy on foreign investments was discussed already in Chapter 1 in connection with investment climate. It was seen there how hard this concept is to operationalize and compare. All the different rules must be weighted differently depending on the project considered. Implementation of the rules varies tremendously. Also differing are the times between the passing of the laws and their implementation. All this would be a good subject for a whole new research project, but it is not possible here because of limits on time and resources (compare Ayres 1975, p. 27).

The importance of government transfers, especially when these coincide with a change in the perceived color of the government, has been demonstrated. But it has not been possible to demonstrate anything about the importance of policy changes that occur independently of changes in political stability.

LEVEL OF THE FLOW OF INVESTMENTS

The only concern so far has been in explaining the trend change in the flow of foreign investments. In this section the level of these flows between years of trend changes will be discussed.

The average number of subsidiaries established per year was calculated for the periods with the same level of investments, that is, between changes in the trend. Because of the increase in investments over time and of the difficulties in obtaining valid and reliable economic data for earlier years, only time periods starting around 1958 or later were included in the analysis. For each time period the average for some of the economic variables discussed earlier in this chapter and the political event summary indices were calculated to be used as independent variables. Gross National Product (GNP) and GNP per capita were also added as independent variables (*World Handbook* 1972). Data restrictions permitted only the six Latin American and the three European countries to be analyzed.

Each period includes a different number of years. If a single year period began by the same type of trend change as either the period before or after, it was included into that period. Further, the number of periods is different for each country. To control for this, the periods were also weighted so that each country had the same influence on the result. This did not change the results. It was also tried to include the year before the trend change since the earlier results had shown the importance of these years. But the results were very similar whether this was done or not.

Step-wise regression analysis was done on this data set. The resulting equations show that, as expected, market size, measured by the GNP, is the most powerful variable for explaining the level of the investment flow (Table 5.3). (The GNP values for 1960 were used, which may have biased the result.) The second variable entered into the equation was the type of trend change, positive or negative, that began the period. The third variable, with a negative beta, was the average number of government instability events per year during the period. With these three independent variables, 62 percent of the variation in level of the investment flow between the periods has been explained. If only the political variables were included the first variable to enter was ln deaths, the second mass political violence, having a positive beta. This is probably due to the high level of mass political events reported in France. If data was missing for one year the average value for the rest of the years was assigned to that year.

This result validates the method used in Chapter 4. Assuming that no new trend changes occur, one can predict the investment flow by looking at the GNP and the direction of the previous trend change. The assumption of no trend change can be relaxed if we predict the trend changes. In Chapter 4 a large step in this direction was taken by showing the importance of political events and especially government events to these trend changes.

TABLE 5.3

Step-wise Regression Equation of the Average Number of Investments During the Periods between Trend Changes

Independent variable	beta	F
GNP	.75	26.34
Trend change type*	.54	22.29
Government instability	−.30	4.27

Note: $R^2 = .62; N = 33; F = 15.98$.

*A dummy variable, where positive trend change = 1, negative trend change = 0.

Source: Data compiled by the author from the Harvard Business School's Multinational Enterprise project data bank, the *World Handbook* data file, and the International Monetary Fund, *Balance of Payments Yearbook*.

6

DIFFERENCES BETWEEN TYPES OF INDUSTRIES AND MARKETS

INTRODUCTION

In Part I three hypotheses on differences between industries were derived. The first of these stated that the higher the degree of oligopoly, the weaker the relationship between investments and political events. The second said that the relationship is stronger in labor-intensive industries than in others. The last one stated that large-scale industries will decrease their investments relatively fast while increasing them relatively slowly.

The industry characteristics were operationalized in Chapter 3. There it could be seen that when the industries were divided according to scale, labor-intensity, and concentration the large scale, low labor-intensity and high concentration groups to a large extent overlapped. The same was of course true for the small-scale, high labor-intensity, and low-concentration groups. This will make it hard to differentiate between the hypotheses when testing them, especially since the small sample makes multivariate analysis impossible. This, coupled with the fact that two of the hypotheses make the same prediction, means that the result from the analysis below will be very preliminary.

When this study was designed, it was thought that regression analysis could be used to compare the investment behavior in different industries, in and from different countries, and so on. It would then have been able to compare the regression coefficients. But as shown in Chapter 4 it is not possible to make any conclusions based on regression analysis of this data material since among other things the relationship between the variables is asymmetric, that is, the negative and positive reactions are different. This leaves the very crude method used in Chapter 4 when analyzing the differences between industries and between countries.

SCALE

It is to be remembered that hypothesis 6 states that companies in large-scale industries will decrease their investments before companies in small-scale industries, but will increase them after. It is thus expected that for negative trend changes, companies in large-scale industries will use a shorter time lag than companies in small-scale industries, and for positive changes will use a longer time lag, with the assumption that they react to the same events.

Table 6.1 shows the difference between large-scale and small-scale industry investments in three Latin American countries. With regard to the negative changes, the table shows that American companies in large-scale industries react negatively to prolonged government instability, even years after mass political instability. They do not react immediately. U.S. companies in small-scale industries react negatively after all types of events have been high, and mass political instability is high the same year. There is no real difference in timing between the two American groups when they decrease their investments. European corporations in large-scale industries react negatively immediately when all types of events are high, while for European companies in small-scale industries the result is very strange: Almost all events are actually lower both the year of and the year before negative changes. This can be interpreted as a support for the hypothesis, although the result for small-scale industries is very unexpected.

Before positive trend changes for American companies in large-scale industries there have been two years of government instability (the same as for negative changes). When this is compared with small-scale industry companies, it can be seen that for the latter positive changes are associated with government events and mass violence the year before. Again for the U.S. companies there seems to be no difference between companies in large- and small-scale industries in the timing. For the European companies it can be seen that companies in both large- and small-scale industries react positively to government transfers after one year.

In summary it thus can be said that very little support has been found for the hypothesis analyzing the investments in Latin America, but more data needs to be analyzed.

The data for the investments in France, Spain, and Italy is shown in Table 2. As was pointed out in Chapter 4, the investments in these countries have increased since World War II. Therefore two time periods were used when defining trend changes; this analysis will be limited to the second time period, 1958–67, since there are a limited number of observations for large-scale industries during the earlier time period. This might pose some problems of comparability, but these are probably minor.

When the positive changes for these European countries are analyzed it can

TABLE 6.1

Differences between Investments in Large-scale and Small-scale Industries in Mexico, Brazil, and Argentina

Home Country	Industry	Type of Trend Change	Time Lag	Ratios between Mean Frequency of Event Years of Change and Years of No Change			
				Government Transfers	Government Instability	Mass Political Instability	Deaths
United States	large-scale	positive	0	1.05	1.64	1.08	.75
			1	1.27	1.99	.72	.79
		negative	0	.22	1.42	.77	1.22
			1	1.10	1.54	1.13	1.52
	small-scale	positive	0	.30	.65	1.19	.89
			1	1.22	1.41	1.00	1.70
		negative	0	1.02	.84	2.18	.89
			1	1.69	1.76	2.36	1.98
Europe	large-scale	positive	0	.93	.25	.87	.73
			1	1.92	1.28	.79	.34
		negative	0	2.46	1.66	1.43	1.13
			1	.63	.68	.81	.55
	small-scale	positive	0	.88	.80	.72	1.26
			1	1.71	1.02	1.02	.98
		negative	0	0/.64	.23	.73	.71
			1	0/.52	1.02	.62	1.27

Note: 0/XX signifies that there were no events of that type during the years of change, XX being the mean number of that event during the years of no change.

Source: Data compiled by the author from the Harvard Business School's Multinational Enterprise project data bank, the *World Handbook* data file, and the International Monetary Fund, *Balance of Payments Yearbook.*

TABLE 6.2

Differences between Investments in Large-scale and Small-scale Industries in France, Spain, and Italy

Home Country	Industry	Type of Trend Change	Time Lag	Ratios between Mean Frequency of Event Years of Change and Years of No Change			
				Government Transfers	Government Instability	Mass Political Instability	Deaths
United States	large-scale	positive	0	.56	.54	.77	0/.67
			1	1.00	1.23	3.73	1.92
		negative	0	0/.45	.88	2.07	.55
			1	0/.50	1.19	.97	.81
	small-scale	positive	0	.53	.50	.66	0/.69
			1	1.60	.76	.46	.89
		negative	0	0/.47	.50	.51	.51
			1	0/.47	.16	.31	0/.76
Europe	large-scale	positive	0	4.76	1.88	.41	.93
			1	2.03	.69	.42	.70
		negative	0	2.38	2.60	.52	0/.64
			1	1.35	1.73	.33	0/.79
	small-scale	positive	0	.65	.90	.82	.56
			1	.52	1.86	.47	.23
		negative	0	0/.44	.36	2.26	.90
			1	0/.56	.62	1.12	0/.88

Note: 0/XX signifies that there were no events of that type during the years of change, XX being the mean number of that event during the years of no change.

Source: Data compiled by the author from the Harvard Business School's Multinational Enterprise project data bank, the *World Handbook* data file, and the International Monetary Fund, *Balance of Payments Yearbook*.

be seen that the American investments increase during calm years both in large- and small-scale industries. But there is some mass political instability the year before large-scale industry companies increase their investments and some government transfers the year before small-scale industry companies change their investment trend upward. For the European companies in large-scale industries, government transfers occur the same year as they increase their investments. European companies in small-scale industries increase their investments when the stability is relatively high, although there has been some government instability the year before the positive trend changes.

For the negative changes American companies in large industries react to the mass political instability the same year, while small-scale companies do not react at all. This is the same result obtained for the European companies in small-scale industries in Latin America. European large-scale corporations react negatively to two years of government events, while companies in small-scale industries react to mass political instability the same year. If there is a difference between the two, it is that large-scale companies react more slowly.

No support has been found for hypothesis 6, which states "Companies in industries where large amounts of capital are needed for an investment will react relatively quickly when a country becomes more unstable, and relatively slowly when a country becomes more stable." But the analysis has shown that negative trend changes often are more strongly associated with political events for companies in large-scale industries than for companies in small-scale industries. When the distance is far between host and home countries it is even found that for companies in small-scale industries there is no relationship between political events and for negative changes in the investment trend. It is harder to see any pattern in the differences between the industries for positive trend changes. Compared with the results in Chapter 4, the results seem rather stable, especially considering that the years of change are not by definition the same when we disaggregate and the shorter time period used in this chapter for France, Spain, and Italy.

Before ending this section another way of testing hypothesis 6 will be discussed. Hypothesis 6 stated that companies in both large- and small-scale industries react to political events but that large-scale companies decrease their investments before, and increase them after, small-scale companies. This is the same as saying that the correlation between the two groups' investment changes should be highest with the investment changes of small-scale companies lagged behind the investment changes of large-scale companies when the investment decreases. The correlation should be highest with the investment changes of large-scale industries lagged behind those of small-scale industries when the investment increases. This was tested for European and U.S. investments in Mexico, Brazil, Argentina, France, Italy, and Spain using Pearson's correlation for each country separately. There was no pattern at all in the way the coefficients were distributed. This result can be due to the fact that other factors have large and different effects on the different groups. Or it can be due to the fact that all the changes, and not only trend changes, are analyzed.

This supports the earlier conclusion. It has not been possible to find the differences between large-scale and small-scale industries that we expected.

LABOR INTENSITY

Hypothesis 5 states that, "The relationship between investments and political stability is stronger, ceteris paribus, for companies in highly labor-intensive industries than for companies in industries that are not labor-intensive." The question then is how to decide that companies in the industry react more strongly than companies in another industry with the method used. The ratios show the proportion of the events that happen during years of (or before) trend changes, in comparison with the years of no change. If the ratio is higher, this means that a higher proportion of the events has happened during this type of year. This also means that the reaction is stronger, since the companies really react to high frequencies of these events. The same is true for absence of events. The problem, however, is that both the current year and the year before are analyzed. Which is to react more strongly: to react promptly the same year, but less; or to react more the next year? In other words, how shall promptness be weighed against size? This question is very hard to answer, so each case must be investigated separately.

Table 6.3 shows the difference between companies in high- and low-intensity industries in Mexico, Brazil, and Argentina. U.S. companies in low labor-intensive industries increase their investment relatively weakly and late to government events. The ratios for companies in high labor-intensity industries on the other hand are almost all higher than 1 both for the same year and the year earlier. This means that high labor-intensity industry companies react strongly but not until they have experienced a longer period of disturbances. For decreases the result for the U.S. companies is mixed. It cannot be said that corporations in high labor-intensity industries are more sensitive than corporations in low labor-intensity industries; both seem to react one year after many of the events, especially when transfers have been high. No major differences between European companies in high and low labor-intensity industries for positive trend changes can be found. For negative changes high labor-intensity industry companies seem to react faster to transfers, while low labor-intensity industry companies react later but more strongly. The latter also decreases its investments strongly and immediately after protests.

Very little support for the hypothesis has been found so far, but this might be because countries where export is of minor importance such as Brazil and Argentina have been included. Therefore an analysis was done of Mexico alone where many investments have been made to exploit cheap labor. The time

TABLE 6.3

Differences between Investments in High and Low Labor-Intensity Industries in Mexico, Brazil, and Argentina

Home Country	Industry	Type of Trend Change	Time Lag	Ratios between Mean Frequency of Event Years of Change and Years of No Change			
				Government Transfers	Government Instability	Mass Political Instability	Deaths
United States	large-scale	positive	0	.46	.56	.90	.18
			1	1.19	1.48	.83	.63
		negative	0	.79	1.72	.85	1.65
			1	2.60	2.01	1.85	.85
	small-scale	positive	0	1.22	1.28	1.82	1.09
			1	1.24	1.63	1.22	.86
		negative	0	1.15	1.19	1.14	1.02
			1	2.22	2.51	1.78	1.48
Europe	large-scale	positive	0	1.40	.75	.22	.89
			1	2.55	1.49	1.06	.75
		negative	0	0/.57	0/1.06	2.30	1.74
			1	2.13	1.06	.27	0/1.85
	small-scale	positive	0	1.04	.82	.79	1.09
			1	2.69	1.43	.78	1.18
		negative	0	1.51	.95	.90	.71
			1	.35	.33	1.00	1.17

Note: 0/XX signifies that there were no events of that type during the years of change, XX being the mean number of that event during the years of no change.

Source: Data compiled by the author from the Harvard Business School's Multinational Enterprise project data bank, the *World Handbook* data file, and the International Monetary Fund, *Balance of Payments Yearbook.*

period is limited to 1955–67 since this phenomenon has gained in importance since World War II. The result is shown in Table 6.4.

The table shows that companies in low labor-intensity industries investing in Mexico react very quickly and relatively strongly. The positive reaction occurs the same year as instability is high. This is contrary to the results for Mexico, Brazil, and Argentina as a group. Companies in high labor-intensity industries react negatively to a prolonged period of a high level of disturbances. The positive changes occur in years of government instability and mass political instability.

Obviously hypothesis 5 on the basis of these results has be be rejected. When Mexico alone was analyzed, the results were biased in favor of country-specific factors of a particular country, Mexico. Had it been possible to study a whole group of this type of country, the results might have been different. For example: What has been seen from the analysis above is the overwhelming importance of government events and especially transfers for all countries. This was not true when only Mexico was analyzed, but this can probably be explained very easily by government stability, that is, the same party has been in power in Mexico during the whole time period.

In order to try to generate some more information investments in Europe have been analyzed (Table 6.5). U.S. investments in France, Spain, and Italy in low labor-intensive industries increase in calm years, after years of government transfers. Decreases also happen in calm years. In high labor-intensive industries investments increase in calm years, but decrease in years of instability, and especially during mass political instability.

European investments in the same countries and in low labor-intensive industries increase during years when there is some instability and decreases happen during years of very high government instability. The result is similar for high labor-intensive industries, but not so pronounced.

The result for the U.S. companies thus weakly supports hypothesis 5, while the results of the European companies are totally contradictory.

When these results are compared to those for the Latin American countries it is impossible to detect any pattern in the differences between low and high labor-intensive industries that justifies a new hypothesis.

DEGREE OF CONCENTRATION

Companies in an oligopolistic situation react more to each other's behavior than to changes in the environment. Hypothesis 3 states that companies in highly concentrated industries are less sensitive to political events, that is, "The higher the degree of oligopoly in the industry in which the company is, the weaker the relationship between political stability and foreign investment." The data for the three Latin American countries shows that this is obviously

TABLE 6.4

Differences between U.S. Investments in High and Low Labor-intensive Industries in Mexico

Home Country	Industry	Type of Trend Change	Time Lag	Ratio between Mean Frequency of Event Years of Change and Years of No Change			
				Government Transfers	Government Instability	Mass Political Instability	Deaths
United States	low labor-intensive	positive	0	3.00	.75	1.06	.30
			1	0/.22	0/.56	.47	.47
		negative	0	0/.11	0/.44	1.02	1.52
			1	0/.22	0/.56	.17	0/2.94
	high labor-intensive	positive	0	0/.22	2.27	2.79	1.05
			1	0/.22	0/.44	1.19	.94
		negative	0	0/.22	4.55	2.02	1.33
			1	0/.22	1.14	2.56	1.7/0

Note: 0/XX signifies that there were no events of that type during the years of change, XX being the mean number of that event during the years of no change; XX/0 signifies that there were no events of that type during the years of no change, XX being the mean number of that event during the years of change.

Source: Data compiled by the author from the Harvard Business School's Multinational Enterprise project data bank, the *World Handbook* data file, and the International Monetary Fund, *Balance of Payments Yearbook.*

TABLE 6.5

Differences between Investments in High and Low and Labor-Intensive Industries in France, Spain, and Italy

Home Country	Industry	Type of Trend Change	Time Lag	Ratios between Mean Frequency of Event Years of Change and Years of No Change			
				Government Transfers	Government Instability	Mass Political Instability	Deaths
United States	low labor-intensive	positive	0	.66	.53	.79	.26
			1	1.89	1.01	.56	1.11
		negative	0	0/.50	.55	1.37	.74
			1	0/.44	.27	.49	0/.76
	high labor-intensive	positive	0	.76	.59	1.20	0/.36
			1	.41	.46	.45	0/.84
		negative	0	1.82	1.31	2.79	4.44
			1	0/.61	.29	1.41	.52
Europe	low labor-intensive	positive	0	1.21	1.52	.69	0/.69
			1	1.05	1.10	.59	1.11
		negative	0	3.03	8.70	.37	0/.69
			1	5.26	2.21	.70	0/.65
	high labor-intensive	positive	0	1.18	.74	.64	.73
			1	.59	1.46	.39	0/.90
		negative	0	3.57	1.02	.54	1.33
			1	0/.56	.26	.64	.41

Note: 0/XX signifies that there were no events of that type during the years of change, XX being the mean number of that event during the years of no change.

Source: Data compiled by the author from the Harvard Business School's Multinational Enterprise project data bank, the *World Handbook* data file, and the International Monetary Fund, *Balance of Payments Yearbook*.

not true. Almost all the ratios are higher for companies in high-concentration industries than for companies in low-concentration industries. The hypothesis must be rejected and some indications have been found that the opposite might be true. (See Table 6.6)

As mentioned in Part I this might be due to the effect of the combination of reaction to changes in the environment and oligopolistic behavior. An oligopoly as a whole does not invest until the environment is perceived as good, but as soon as one company reacts to a change in the environment, then the others will follow, that is, a strong reaction follows. Especially in less developed countries where markets can still be opened up, oligopolistic behavior complements the natural drive for markets, meaning the reaction will be stronger for companies in high- than low-concentration industries. The new hypothesis, then, is as follows.

Hypothesis 3a:
The higher the degree of oligopoly in an industry, the stronger the relationship between political stability and foreign investments, since the oligopolistic behavior will reinforce the normal reaction to changes in political stability.

This new hypothesis is supported in Knickerbocker's results, which showed the importance of the environment for the oligopolistic reaction. Knickerbocker summarized his results in the following way:

By showing a positive relationship between the intensity of oligopolistic reaction and country stability, they [the results] indicate that oligopolists were not inclined to make defensive investments in unstable markets (Knickerbocker 1972, p. 184).

In contrast to Knickerbocker, who looked at long-term stability, the importance of short-term stability has been shown here. Strictly speaking only a correlation between investment changes and political events in oligopolistic industries has been shown. It is possible that government policies are the deciding factor—an intervening variable. It is in oligopolistic industries that governments often are especially active in trying to develop their countries for example, through inviting companies to start production and at the same time raising the tariffs for the product.

Thus, with regard to the data for France, Spain, and Italy (see Table 6.7) there are two alternative hypotheses. Both U.S. and European companies in low-concentration industries increase their investments in France, Spain, and Italy during years of government events, especially transfers. Companies in high-concentration industries on the other hand increase during calm years for the European companies in combination with government events the year before.

TABLE 6.6

Differences between Investments in High and Low Concentration Industries in Mexico, Brazil, and Argentina

Home Country	Industry	Type of Trend Change	Time Lag	Ratios between Mean Frequency of Event Years of Change and Years of No Change			
				Government Transfers	Government Instability	Mass Political Instability	Deaths
United States	high-concentrated	positive	0	2.92	3.16	1.85	.75
			1	2.44	2.11	1.01	.74
		negative	0	1.40	2.41	1.53	1.23
			1	2.85	2.86	1.90	1.19
	low-concentrated	positive	0	.48	.68	.73	.79
			1	.25	.75	.84	1.46
		negative	0	1.12	1.11	.60	1.47
			1	1.82	1.58	1.50	1.82
Europe	high-concentrated	positive	0	.60	.67	1.04	.89
			1	3.27	2.13	.69	1.08
		negative	0	2.42	1.07	2.05	1.29
			1	0/.51	.71	1.33	.88
	low-concentrated	positive	0	1.25	1.18	.60	1.11
			1	1.19	.86	1.30	.83
		negative	0	.89	.66	.84	.52
			1	0/.59	.64	.78	1.17

Note: 0/XX signifies that there were no events of that type during the years of change, XX being the mean number of that event during the years of no change.

Source: Data compiled by the author from the Harvard Business School's Multinational Enterprise project data bank, the *World Handbook* data file, and the International Monetary Fund, *Balance of Payments Yearbook*.

TABLE 6.7

Differences between Investments in High and Low Concentration Industries in France, Spain, and Italy

Home Country	Industry	Type of Trend Change	Time Lag	Ratios between Mean Frequency of Event Years of Change and Years of No Change			
				Government Transfers	Government Instability	Mass Political Instability	Deaths
United States	high-concentration	positive	0	.73	.66	.80	0/.67
			1	.60	.67	.73	0/.76
		negative	0	0/.45	.16	1.12	.42
			1	0/.55	.28	.56	.60
	low-concentration	positive	0	1.59	1.07	.94	4.13
			1	1.20	.80	.66	.72
		negative	0	2.22	1.44	3.45	10.07
			1	0/.50	.28	1.27	.37
Europe	high-concentration	positive	0	0/.40	.50	.22	0/.54
			1	1.91	3.48	.32	0/.65
		negative	0	0/.40	.25	1.88	2.04
			1	5.71	3.96	.76	3.69
	low-concentration	positive	0	2.63	1.94	.81	.55
			1	1.32	2.33	.54	.58
		negative	0	5.26	5.17	1.90	2.00
			1	1.76	1.65	1.25	.47

Note: 0/XX signifies that there were no events of that type during the years of change, XX being the mean number of that event during the years of no change.

Source: Data compiled by the author from the Harvard Business School's Multinational Enterprise project data bank, the *World Handbook* data file, and the International Monetary Fund, *Balance of Payments Yearbook.*

Decreases occur in years of, and after, high levels of all events. This is especially true for companies in low-concentration industries that react somewhat faster and more strongly than companies in high-concentration industries.

The results for these three European countries support the original hypothesis 3 that companies in low-concentration industries react more strongly to political events than companies in high-concentration industries. Perhaps the difference between Latin America and Europe can be explained by the government characteristics found in Chapter 4. In Latin America, government events are much more important both for positive and negative trend changes than in Europe. Political events are more important to highly concentrated industries in Latin America, while in Europe, political events are of less importance to those industries. It was speculated that this is because the markets are in different stages of development in the two regions. In Europe the markets are older and already penetrated by the oligopolies, while in Latin America the markets are new and relatively little penetrated. There new markets can still be opened up, for example by a government decree.

IMPORTANCE OF MARKET SIZE

In Part I hypothesis 4 was presented that companies would be more sensitive to political events in small markets than in large markets, namely, "The bigger the market and/or market growth a country has, the weaker the relationship, ceteris paribus, between political stability and foreign direct investment in that country." When comparing two groups of countries divided according to one characteristic, it is desirable that they be as similar as possible in all other respects to the one being compared. But since it is impossible to find two countries that are exactly similar, this problem has to be solved by taking more than two countries and grouping them together. As much as possible must be kept constant, and it is hoped that the effect of all other factors evens out.

This hypothesis will be tested on American investments in Latin America. Brazil and Argentina make up the large-market group, and Chile and Colombia make up the small-market group. By taking only American investments and Latin American countries, it is hoped that as much as possible has been kept constant, although these countries are different in many respects.

Table 6.8 shows that in Brazil and Argentina the negative reaction is very strong after one year, while the reaction is much weaker and quicker in Chile-Colombia. The positive reaction is also much stronger in the large-market countries.

The findings, contrary to the original hypothesis, are that companies react more strongly to political events in large markets than in small markets. But at the same time, probably because the stakes are much higher, the companies are slower to reduce their investments in the large-market countries.

TABLE 6.8

Differences between U.S. Investments
in Large and Small Markets

	Host Country							
	Brazil-Argentina				Chile-Colombia			
Trend change	pos.	pos.	neg.	neg.	pos.	pos.	neg.	neg.
Time lag	0	1	0	1	0	1	0	1
Government transfers	.84	2.93	.59	3.97	.28	.88	.41	.44
Government instability	1.13	2.94	1.59	4.16	.23	.58	1.33	.29
Mass political instability	.73	1.77	1.23	2.49	1.01	.61	1.35	.52
Deaths	1.21	2.49	1.48	2.25	1.16	1.16	1.31	1.52

Source: Data compiled by the author from the Harvard Business School's Multinational Enterprise project data bank, the *World Handbook* data file, and the International Monetary Fund, *Balance of Payments Yearbook.*

CONCLUSIONS

All the hypotheses tested in this chapter have had to be modified, but as pointed out in the introduction, it should be remembered that they have been tested on a very small number of countries. Only one variable at a time has been studied; in addition, it was not possible to study interactions between variables with the very crude test methods used here. The results are not, and should not be, considered more than new preliminary theses that have to be tested on new data. The results will be summarized in the next chapter.

7

THEORETICAL
CONCLUSIONS

TOWARD A POLITICAL THEORY OF FOREIGN DIRECT INVESTMENT

The forces behind large corprations' decisions to invest abroad were discussed at length in Part I. As was seen there, most theories of foreign direct investment assume the political environment to be constant or totally ignore it.

In summarizing the major findings of this study, it has been found that the investment flow to a country during a specific time period to a large extent can be explained by the Gross National Product of the country, and by the type of major investment trend change, positive or negative, that initiated the period. These trend changes are associated with, if not explained by, certain political events. With the help of the hypotheses tested it is possible to summarize what this association looked like.

Hypothesis 1 stated that "The investments in a country decrease when a country is unstable and increase when it is stable ceteris paribus." This hypothesis, general as it is, seems to be confirmed, but the relationship is not as simple as described in the hypothesis. First, political events, and thus degree of stability, are associated with major trend changes in the investment flow but not directly with real short-term fluctuations. It has been argued that to a large extent this is because the "image" of a country is a very decisive factor, and that this image only changes in connection with major political events. Second, the relationship is asymmetric, that is, the companies do not react in the same way when a country becomes stable as when it is unstable.

Hypothesis 2 said that "Government events will be followed either by an investment increase or decrease, in both cases of larger size than after mass political events." This hypothesis was supported by the data too. Government events seem to be of larger importance than mass political events. It was argued this was probably due to the importance of government policy, especially the color of the government and its general economic policy, but also its policy towards foreign investment.

Turning to the importance of the companies' home countries, hypothesis 7, as follows, was tested: "The closer the relationship between the home country and the potential host country, the weaker the correlation between political stability and investment changes." The difference between American and European companies investing in Latin America and Europe was primarily analyzed. The results seem to indicate that the opposite of hypothesis 7 is true: it is the Americans who react more to political events in Latin America, and Europeans to political events in Europe. This might be caused by differences in efficiency. This conclusion is supported by another finding: When studying the difference between industries it was found that for companies in small-scale industries investing in countries far from home, there is no relationship between political events and the establishment of subsidiaries. One caveat however: It might also be caused by the fact that companies, and perhaps especially small companies, establish themselves when they get one large order that is independent of the political situation.

With regard to hypotheses on differences between industries hypothesis 6 states, "Companies in industries where large amounts of capital are needed for an investment will react relatively quickly when a country becomes more unstable, and relatively slowly when a country becomes more stable." The data did not support this hypothesis, although we found that for negative trend changes the association with political events is somewhat stronger for companies in large-scale industries than in small-scale industries. The second industry hypothesis, hypothesis 5, stated that "The relationship between investments and political stability is stronger, ceteris paribus, for companies in highly labor-intensive industries than for companies in industries that are not labor-intensive." The hypothesis, first tested on Mexico, Brazil, and Argentina and then on Mexico alone, had to be rejected. No alternative hypothesis was able to be formulated, even though the three European countries were also studied.

With reference to the importance of oligopolistic behavior, the hypothesis 3 stated, "The higher the degree of oligopoly in the industry in which the company is, the weaker the relationship between political stability and foreign investment." This is true for the European countries, while in Latin America the opposite seems to be true. It was speculated that this was caused by differences in market penetration by the international oligopolies. As stated in chapter 6: "In less developed countries where markets can still be opened up, oligopolistic behavior complements the natural drive for markets, meaning the reaction will be stronger for companies in high- than low-concentration industries." The alternative hypothesis (3a) valid for Latin America was: "The higher the degree of oligopoly in an industry, the stronger the relationship between political stability and foreign investments, since the oligopolistic behavior will reinforce the normal reaction to changes to political stability."

With reference to the importance of type of host countries, only France, Spain, and Italy together with Mexico, Brazil, and Argentina were able to be compared, because of the method of analysis and the limited number of countries. The differences were interesting: In Europe the negative trend changes seem to be caused directly by mass political instability; general stability per se seems to be enough for investments to increase. In Latin America government instability and especially government transfers are much more important. There is an association with mass political instability, but this is working through government events, so the ultimate consequences of political instability can either be an increase or decrease in the flow of investment from abroad.

A special case of types of host countries is the importance of market characteristics. Hypothesis 4 states that "The larger the market and/or market growth a country has, the weaker the relationship, ceteris paribus, between political stability and foreign direct investment in that country." This was tested on Brazil-Argentina as large markets and Chile-Colombia as small markets. The results indicate that in fact the opposite to the hypothesis seems to be true: the reaction is stronger in large markets. But at the same time companies are slower to reduce their investments in large markets, probably since the opportunity cost of staying out of large markets is potentially very high.

This study has shown that to the traditional economic theories on foreign direct investments one has to add a political theory describing the importance of political events and especially of government events. In this study a first step towards such a theory was taken, although the results are preliminary and tentative. Eventually such a theory will give a much fuller picture of the investment behavior of multinational corporations.

THE MULTINATIONAL CORPORATION AS AN ACTOR

During the last few years multinational corporations have become the object of a very heated debate. The participants in this debate have especially focused on the effects the companies have or may have on different types of countries (Keohane and Van Doorn 1975, pp. 172–86). Multinational corporations have also often been seen as instruments used by one government to manipulate other countries and particularly as tools for neocolonialism and imperialism.

When a unit is studied it can be done in two different ways, either from the environment to the unit—that is, the researcher is primarily interested in the effects of the unit—or the unit itself can be studied. In this case, one studies the unit's behavior and characteristics as such (Sjostedt 1974, p. 7). It is the latter starting point that has been used in this study, since it is necessary first to study a phenomenon itself before one really can say anything about its effects on the environment. This is especially true if the aim is to make predictions about the future.

It is impossible, however, to study the total behavior of all units of a certain type. The necessary limitations can be made either by reducing the number of units studied or by keeping the number of units high but instead reducing the types of behavior studied. In the first case one does case studies; as examples of this approach are Sampson's study of ITT (Sampson 1973), and Goodsell's study of (especially) the international Petroleum Company in Peru (Goodsell 1974). The problem with this case approach is that it is extremely hard to get enough detailed information, and it is hard to generalize the results to other units. Generalization to other similar units is much easier when one studies a relatively high number of units, but then the problem is instead to generalize to other types of behavior. If behavior that is normal to the unit is chosen this problem can be minimized. It is this latter approach that has been used in this study.

The decision to invest abroad occurs regularly in any large multinational corporation; it is processed through the normal system for corporate decisions, and within the corporation it is regarded as an economic decision. This makes the decision to invest abroad a very good type of behavior to study.

In this section we will try to summarize how corporations behave as actors in the international system. First, however, we must define what we mean by actor and an actor's behavior.

Is the Multinational Corporation an Actor?

Sjostedt has argued that "Two basic requirements have in principle to be fully met if a certain unit can be classified as a full-fledged actor" (Sjostedt 1974, p. 5). First the unit must have a minimal level of autonomy, that is, it must be possible to differentiate between the unit and its environment. And secondly the unit's "behavior" must have an impact on its environment (Sjostedt 1974, p. 5). It is obvious without any deeper analysis that large multinational corporations fulfill these requirements. As mentioned above, these are two of the main questions in the debate on multinational corporations, and there are many studies of the impact of these corporations on nations, labor unions, competitors, consumer groups, and so forth. Although it is clear that large multinational corporations are actors, as defined by these requirements, it is hard to draw the line as to when a company is not an actor. In a totally free market without imperfections one can hardly say that the companies are actors since their behavior is totally determined by the market. This was discussed at length in Chapter 1.

In this study the problem was circumvented by choosing a number of large corporations well inside this line. That is, they were very large corporations, often in oligopolistic industries with activities in many countries.

But there is still some ambiguity as to how a company shall be differentiated from its environment: When, for example, is a firm part of another actor (as a subsidiary), and when is it an actor on its own? In reality this probably differs from situation to situation. In Part I, for example, the importance of internal politics within the corporation was shown. In the empirical part of this study the definition of a company established by the Harvard Multinational Enterprise Project was used. There are, of course, many other definitions of a corporation, that is, an actor, that could have been used.

Besides fulfilling these two basic requirements, the unit also has to show actor behavior, which "may in general terms be described as transactions from the [corporation] to its international environment" (Sjostedt 1974, p. 8). These transactions involve things such as goods, services, capital, and so on. Corporations certainly have transactions with their environments, but not all transactions should be called actor behavior. "Transaction(s) should conform with the interest of the [corporation] with respect to contents, form, means, transmitter and recipient" (Sjostedt 1974, p. 12). The problem comes down to defining "interest." There is a whole literature in political science showing how difficult that is, but there seems to be two general approaches to it. The first is to define interest "Objectively," through a theory, for example Marxist theory. The second is to study internal documents and interview people, to get a "subjective" definition. In doing this, one has to be aware that a correlation between interest and behavior can be spurious. For example, the multinational corporation is often accused of being used as an instrument by its home government (or host government, as during the oil crisis) to influence other actors. In this case, one can hardly say that the multinational corporation is an actor if it does something that is against its own interest. The borderline gets very blurred, however, since there can be a trade off for the corporation between the result of following the government's wishes and what would happen otherwise.

For discussion of the MNC as an instrument see Nye (1974, p. 154). Nye has argued that multinational firms can play three different roles in international politics: The direct role (private foreign policy); the unintended direct role (instruments of influence); the indirect role (setting the agenda). In the last category Nye includes lobbying for certain trade agreements (Nye 1974, p. 154 ff.). It can be argued that this should be included in the first category, especially if the company's policy is regarded as global. That is the way it has been treated in this text. For the last category, Nye points at three ways the companies can do this unintentionally: first, through being the object of dispute between countries as regards such things as antitrust, or taxation; second, in the effect their activities have on trade and money; and third, through stimulating other social groups to press for certain government policies. The foreign direct investment fits into the second way.

The problem of defining an actor is similar to the problem already discussed of making a distinction between politics and economics. In the long run this is almost impossible, since the regime for economic interactions and markets is dependent upon political sanctions.

Still, it is absolutely clear from this discussion that large multinational corporations can be viewed and studied as political actors. This conclusion is supported by the fact that although there are other definitions of actors than the one used here, there are very few people who dispute that a multinational corporation at least has the ability to be an actor in the international political system.

The Multinational Corporation as a Political Actor

The decision to invest abroad is a normal and routine decision within the company and it is thus possible to a certain extent at least to generalize these results into other types of activities that large corporations engage in. This in turn gives the opportunity to compare the multinational corporation as an actor with other actors in the international system.

This study has shown that multinational corporations as actors are similar to other actors in the international system in many respects. The same things that are found in studies of other actors' decisions have shown up here too. In Part I the importance of organization behavior and bureaucratic politics could already be seen. The empirical analysis has shown the importance of the decision makers' perception on the outcome of the decision to invest abroad. The same conclusions have been drawn in many studies of other actors in the international system.

The decision to invest abroad and the variation in the outcome of this decision process according to differences in the political situation in the potential host country can be characterized as environmental adaptation. The opposite of this would be environmental creation which occurs when companies actively try to change their environments to their advantage through lobbying, bribes, and so forth. (The choice between the two is a strategic one.) Following Nye's classification this would be "the direct role: private foreign policy" (Nye 1974, p. 155). One of the major findings of this study is that even if the corporations engage only in adaption to the environment, they will have very important effects on the environment, especially if a dynamic perspective is taken. Put in other words, the way corporations adapt to their environments today will help to shape the environment tomorrow.

It has been shown that corporations prefer to invest in countries that are perceived as being stable and having a good investment climate. Unfortunately this often means that the companies will, independent of their intentions, support authoritarian and reactionary regimes. This is also the basic argument in Rosen (1974) and Keohane and Van Doorn (1975, p. 180). This study has thus shown another side of the multinational corporation as a political actor than the one that is normally discussed in the debate on this subject. In Nye's terms, the investing corporations will not only set the agenda in a certain way in the short run but will influence the future agendas in the broadest sense of the word. With the increasing resources the multinational corporations control, this aspect of their normal behavior might be of crucial importance.

8

NORMATIVE ASPECTS

IMPLICATIONS FOR MANAGERS OF MULTINATIONAL CORPORATIONS

It is hard to make normative statements from an empirical study like the one presented here. But it is an important part of social science research to try to see the practical implications of research results. Empirical analysis here has shown the relationship between variations in political stability and the establishment of manufacturing subsidiaries by large multinational corporations. The relationship differed according to type of stability, industry, and home country, and host country. What are the normative implications of this?

One thing that must be avoided when trying to see the normative implications of empirical result is to say that since we found most companies doing one thing, all companies should do this. That is obviously not true. There is the possibility that companies behave the way they do because they are forced to by changes in the environment. But the relationship might also be due to subjective factors, since executives perceive changes in the environment in a certain way and act accordingly. The big question is whether there should exist a relationship between the changes in the environment and the companies' behavior or not. This question cannot be answered from the empirical evidence presented, but from the theoretical discussion and the empirical analysis together it seems plausible that the relationship should exist. The discussion below will be based on the following assumption: There should be a relationship between the degree of political stability and the corporation's investment behavior. But note that nothing is assumed about the characteristics of this relationship. Differences in the reactions of two groups of companies could, as seen above, be due to either a difference in efficiency of evaluating the political risk, given that the two groups are equally dependent upon the political factors, or due to a difference in the dependence upon the political situation given the same efficiency of the two groups. For the normative discussion below it will assumed that companies have about the same efficiency. Differences in the reactions will thus be considered due to variations in dependence on the political situation. This will give the basis needed for the normative discussion: If a company is more dependent, it is more important for it to try to evaluate and forecast the political situation.

Our task in this section is to analyze the differences found between groups of companies from this perspective. Some methods of improving the analysis of political risk will also be analyzed.

There is one caveat: There are of course also differences in efficiency. For example, for companies in small-scale industries investing far from home, there is no relationship between political stability and investment behavior. Since there is a relationship for companies in the same industries investing in countries closer to home, the difference is probably due to lack of efficiency. The normative implication of this is obvious.

Normative Statements

It was found in the empirical analysis that companies in high labor-intensive industries are more sensitive to political instability than companies in low labor-intensive industries. Assuming that the companies are equally efficient, we know that companies in high labor-intensive industries are more dependent on political changes. Managers of companies in those industries should therefore place greater importance on political factors than managers in other industries.

Corporations in highly oligopolistic situations are very sensitive to political events in Latin America, but less so in Europe. This implies that managers of companies in oligopolistic industries should pay a lot of attention to the political developments in less-developed countries, especially those countries moving from less stable to more stable. It can be very expensive only to follow the leader, since the bargaining position is very different after one of the companies in the oligopoly has entered. It pays to be first.

Looking at differences between countries it was found that mass political instability has a direct negative impact on companies in Europe. The companies tend to increase their investments during stable periods. Therefore, mass political stability is what managers should keep their eyes on in the European countries.

In Latin American and other less developed countries, on the other hand, the direct importance of mass political instability is relatively low. But there violence tends to occur together with government events and these are very important. The policy of the new government can be totally different from the one of the previous government. Therefore, government stability is extremely important to the investing companies; the possibilities for investments are totally dependent upon the government in power.

Regarding market size, the results imply that companies are more dependent upon the political events in large markets, so it is there managers should concentrate their attention (which they probably already do). This conclusion is supported by the fact that companies tend to tolerate a higher level of instability and still invest in large markets rather than in small markets.

Companies react differently depending upon whether the political instability is increasing or decreasing. The relationship is assymetric. Assuming efficiency in the corporation decisions, the company's dependency varies with the direction of the change in political instability. Finally, it should be stressed that it has been found here that different political events affect specific companies very differently. In Chapter 1, in discussion of political risk, it was argued that a political change may have a negative impact on one company while giving another an opportunity. This is supported by the findings on the importance of government policy. The managers ought to be aware of the impact on their corporations, or parts of them, of potential changes in political stability.

POLITICAL RISK EVALUATION

In this section some strategies for handling political risk will be discussed and an example shown of one company executing a strategy to minimize its political exposure. Then some trends concerning recent disputes between companies and host governments will be observed. Last, one way of analyzing political risk as a bargaining game between the company and the host government will be shown.

Strategies for Handling Political Risk

In Part I, three complementary strategies for handling political risk were mentioned: risk aversion, risk transfer, and risk adaption.

Aversion meant that the management tried to stay away from any political risk. It is obvious that this strategy is most relevant before the investment is made. The simplest way to follow a risk aversion strategy would be to classify all countries in two groups; one where the company invests and one where it never invests. Although it is a very crude method, it is used by many corporations. But there are many other possible, more sophisticated methods (Stobaugh 1969(b) pp. 101–07). The first would be to require a premium for risk, for example by asking for a higher rate of return on investments in high risk countries.

The second method—interval estimation—would mean that the decision maker studies the variables that he considers relevant and that can affect profitability. He can then check what happens when these variables are assigned different values enabling him to obtain the range for the investments' profitability.

The third method—risk analysis—is the most advanced. With the assistance of probability theory and decision trees, the manager can obtain a probability for each possible outcome for the profitability. Then of course it is possible to do sensitivity analysis on this result to see how it varies for different probabilities. A study using this method has, for example, been done by Rothberg (1975) on the crude oil supply risk.

The strategy of transferring risks can be used either before the investment is made, or later, to decrease the political risk for an already existing investment. There are many different methods for transferring risks. Many companies have insurance against losses because of war, inconvertibility and expropriation by the Overseas Private Investment Corporation (OPIC), or similar government organizations in other countries. After the U.S. Congress' decision to "privatize" those insurance programs, many private insurance companies, like Lloyds of London, intensified their attempts to write this kind of insurance. Political risk insurance is expensive—2 to 3 percent for one investment in a high risk country or 0.5 to 0.6 percent for a package including investments in developed countries too. These insurance programs do not protect against war and they are often renegotiated every year (Haendel, West, and Meadow 1975).

There are other methods of transferring the risk, too, one of which is accomplished through consortia, which means that the risk can be spread. Banks lending to less developed countries sometimes also have a cross-default agreement with a development bank, like the World Bank, which means that if the country defaults the flow of money from the development bank will be jeopardized.

The third strategy used is adaption: the company tries to reduce sources of conflict with the host government as much as possible. When considering an investment the management can find it useful to try to evaluate the project from the host country's viewpoint: What effect will the project have on the balance of payments, and on employment? Is the project socially desirable? And so forth. This makes it much easier to assess the political risk and the company's situation. If a company follows a strategy of adaption, it should try to maximize those positive effects, minimize possible negative effects, and try to foresee demands by the government.

An Illustration: Kennecott in Chile

An interesting example of how these three strategies work together is Theodore Moran's study of Kennecott in Chile (Moran 1973). Even though Kennecott is an extractive company, the strategy is valid for manufacturing companies too. Kennecott had had a copper mine in Chile for a long time, but had not invested more than for depreciation since Chile was considered a high-risk country. In the late 1950s, a large investment was necessary to keep the production even at its then present level. Feasibility studies were promising, but Kennecott's management was willing to make the investment only if a "network of transnational alliances could be constructed to protect the company's position" (Moran 1973, p. 277). The strategy Kennecott followed to protect itself in case of nationalization had the following aims: minimizing the cost for Kennecott; maximizing the number of supporters who would automatically share the burden with Kennecott; and maximizing the cost for Chile.

The demand for "Chileanization" by the Frei government in 1964 gave Kennecott the opportunity to implement this strategy. Kennecott offered to sell 51 percent of El Tiente, the copper mine, to the Chilean government, and run the mine through a management contract. As a part of this agreement it was decided that the mine should be expanded. The capital for the expansion came from the government's payments for its part, plus a loan from the American Export-Import Bank. The book value was then revaluated so that "From a balance-sheet perspective . . . Kennecott would still be 49 percent owner of a company worth about 4 times as much as it had been before" (Moran 1973, p. 278). From a cash flow perspective the increase was substantial too. Kennecott then insured this higher value with the U.S. Agency for International Development (AID), the predecessor to OPIC.

Kennecott's management also insisted that the prize paid by Chile for its part of the mine and the loan from the U.S. Export-Import Bank should be guaranteed by the Chilean government and submitted to the law of New York State. All this meant that in case of a nationalization the Export-Import Bank, AID, and the U.S. Congress (through the Hickenlooper amendment) would automatically be parties in the dispute.

To further improve its position, Kennecott then wrote long-term contracts for the output from the mine with European and Asian customers. The collecting rights for these contracts were then sold to a consortium of European banks and a Japanese consortium.

In the dispute following the nationalization by the Allende government, Kennecott was in a very good position and lost very little, while Anaconda, which had done very little to decrease its political risk, lost substantially.

A Note on the Recent History of Takeovers

The number of disputes where American foreign investments have been involved that may result in the disposition of property have increased during the last few years. During just the period July 1971 to July 1973 there were 87 instances of "expropriation or nationalization, intervention, requisition, contract or concession cancellation or renegotiation, and coerced sale" (*Disputes* 1974, p. i). Fifty-six older disputes were still unsolved in the beginning of the period. In these 143 disputes, 39 countries were involved, the largest group being the Latin American countries. Of the 79 Latin American disputes 38 concerned Chile. Most of the disputes were related to raw materials (*Disputes* 1974, pp. 1–7).

What is really interesting is that a shift in the mode of takeover can be observed. A comparison of the new and the old disputes shows that an increasing number of countries have abandoned nationalizations and expropriations as a method for takeover. There is a reason for this is, according to a U.S. State department report:

> ... international law governing formal expropriations is—by reason of extensive precedent—reasonably clear, providing for prompt, adequate and effective compensation. By adopting methods which result in less determinate legal positions LDS's can often enhance the possibilities of an eventual settlement favorable to their interests (*Disputes* 1974, pp 6–7)

This plus the often negative impact of publicity makes it more effective to use low-key administrative measures, and this is probably what managers of multinational corporations have to be prepared to deal with in the future. Nationalizations are still used, however. Truitt (1970, p. 29) argues that "the straightforward, standard form of expropriation and nationalization is not yet extinct and not really significantly diminishing in frequency or magnitude."

The Bargaining Game

The interplay between government and company can be described as a bargaining game, where the government has one thing to offer and the corporation something else. It is a non-zero-sum game. It should be realized that this game and the bargaining strengths of the parties involved is bound to change over time. This will make the probability for a conflict between them very high. A radical change in the bargaining strengths takes place after the corporation has invested in the country. Before investing, the company is very independent of the government; the situation changes very much when the physical investment is in place and the company is committed. An extreme example is seen in a plant that is going to produce for export back to the company's home country (often called off-shore production). The company must try to make as small as possible the change between its situation before and after the investment has been made, perhaps by using the strategies for risk transfers discussed above.

One aspect of this bargaining game is the technological and managerial know-how the investing company brings to the country. Since World War II there has been a clear trend that governments, especially in many less-developed countries, want to control sectors of the economy that are considered vital. The problem is, however, that these sectors tend to be very technologically advanced industries. This gives a clue as to how one might analyze the risk of demands for changes for the control and ownership of the operation.*

The produce-cycle theory states that all products go through a sequence of innovation, growth, and decline. The further in this sequence the product has gone, the more standardized it is and thus the easier to manufacture. At a certain point in time all products can be placed somewhere on the product-cycle curve. At the same time the level of technological and managerial skills that are available in a country decides the level of complexity of products that country can produce. This means that countries can be placed on a sort of product-cycle curve as well. The more advanced the country is, the earlier in the product cycle it is situated. Countries that are less developed will only be able to produce very standardized products. To produce more complicated products the country needs help from abroad, for example in the form of a multinational company investing.

The bargaining situation will thus be very different depending upon whether the product the company produces is more complicated than the host country can manage without external help or not. The point where the country is situated along the product cycle curve can be called the control-frontier.

Taking a dynamic perspective it is obvious that this will lead to conflicts between the country and the investing company. As the products move along the product cycle they will get more standardized, allowing the host country to produce them itself; it does not need the foreign company's know-how any longer. This is reinforced by the country moving its control-frontier in the other direction as it develops. One way the country will get the know-how and learn is through the investing foreign company. Each investment thus contains the seeds of its own destruction from the company's point of view.

---

*The idea for this originates from a lecture given at Harvard University by Professor Raymond Vernon, fall 1975.

The risk of a conflict on control-ownership and/or managerial-ownership could be estimated if each country's "control-frontier" and its rate of movement along the product-cycle curve had been mapped here. It should be pointed out, however, that things are not as easy in practice as they sound in theory. It will be very difficult to do this mapping, especially since the world is changing all the time. The words "industry" and "product" have been used here: the question is not as simple as that. The situation can be very different in varying areas of the industry. The oil industry is a clear example: most countries have now mastered the art of producing raw oil, but they still need the oil companies for refining and especially for off-shore drilling. Perhaps it is better to speak of production processes.

The bargaining positions as defined by the product life-cycle curve will of course be affected by many other factors. For example, corporations in mature oligopolies can have a relatively strong position because they control markets or production. And as has been pointed out, the bargaining situation is very different for the first company in the oligopoly entering the country than for the followers.

PROBABILITY ESTIMATION OF POLITICAL EVENTS

As seen above, all political events should be evaluated normatively in terms of their effects on specific projects and not in general terms. In many cases, the consequences of political events are in fact very small for projects. Effects of a political event could, however, show up in many areas of the project: in production; in the market; in growth, but also through price controls; in management and ownership; in tariffs; and so on. How much these factors have to be analyzed depends upon how important they are considered to be for the project.

Each of the effects mentioned above has to be analyzed separately. Many of them are primarily influenced by economic factors, or can at least be predicted easily in the short run by looking at economic factors. For example, the rules for repatriation of capital are not only dependent on the attitude of the government toward foreign capital but on balance-of-payments consideration. The latter are often more important and sometimes force governments that are very positive to foreign capital to put restrictions on the repatriation of capital.

But once a certain political event has been found to have a potential substantial impact, it then becomes worthwhile to try to estimate the probability of its actually occurring. Also in long-range planning it would be very helpful for decision makers if political conditions could be forecasted. The purpose of this section is to review some of the latest research in political science to see to what extent this is possible. First however, some earlier suggestions on how political risk can be estimated will be examined.

Earlier Models for Political Evaluation

Haner has developed a Business Environmental Risk Index built upon the Delphi technique using a panel to rate the countries each month. The panelists are asked to score the country according to 15 items grouped into three environmental risk subindices: political, operational, and financial (Haendel, West, and Meadow 1975, p. 57). A similar approach is used by *Business International* (1975). The researchers at Business International each year score around 60 countries according to a number of variables grouped into three subindices: political-legal-social factors, commercial factors, and monetary-financial factors. There are certain problems with these indices: they become very subjective and dependent upon the panel; there are serious methodological problems involved, like the arbitrary weighting of the items; there are large validity problems; and finally, there is the problem for which time horizon the risk is relevant or valid. This, latter, is true for most forecasts however (Haendel, West, and Meadow 1975, pp. 57–58).

DuPont is reported to use an interesting approach in which all groups within a country that might influence the policy of that country are identified. The desired policy and the probability of the group affecting government policy is then assessed for each group. This can then be aggregated to give an estimation of the probability function of the government policy (Tugenhat 1972, pp. 173–74). The problem with this approach is that the amount of analysis required is immense. Since it is built on the pluralist theory in political science, it is probably more valid in the developed countries for which that theory is relevant than for developing countries.

Nehrt has developed a model of political climate using policy statements of political leaders and government officials; actions of government, favorable and unfavorable; and the historical context within which the statements and actions took place. Of course this approach assumes that there will be no greater political change in the country (Litvak and Maule 1970, Chpt. 12).

Green has argued that the risk of "radical political change" can be estimated by studying the political structure in the country (Green 1974 b). His scheme, is little more than a taxonomy, however.

The Foreign Policy Research Institute in Philadelphia, which is very active in the area of political risk, has come up with its own "Political System Stability Index" or PSSI. (Haendel, West, and Meadow 1975, pp. 53–72). This index tries to grade the system's stability; it does not try to predict any particular changes or events. It is partly based on some of the theories or findings of the researchers discussed below. But the theoretical foundation for the index is still very weak. Some of the problems concern the causal relationships between different indicators, the question of what the indicator really is measuring, and the dependency on the base time period. Unfortunately many of these problems meet every social scientist trying to construct measures like this. This index can therefore be regarded as a good first step towards a really valid measure.

The most serious problem with this index is, however, that it is very hard to know how this aggregate measure of stability really affects investing corporations. No attempt has been made to study the relationship between this index, conditions for investing companies, and the flow of incoming direct foreign investment.

Measurement of Political Instability

Before the probability of political events is discussed, how these events have been conceptualized and measured by the researchers will first be shown. It is possible to discern two different groups of researchers among those who measure political instability as it is done in this study. One group, the empiricists, use factor analysis to establish different dimensions of political stability. The other group, the theorists, tries instead to build indices by using an explicit theory (Gurr 1973, pp. 359–92).

The first of the empiricists was Rummel, who in a number of studies found three dimensions of domestic conflict behavior: revolution, subversion, and turmoil (Rummel 1963, 1965, 1966). In replications of Rummel's analysis by Tanter (1965; 1966), Borock (quoted in Hazlewood 1973, p. 171) and Wilkinfield (1974), a somewhat different result was obtained. The dimension turmoil was found (strikes, demonstrations, and riots), but Rummel's two other factors were joined into one called internal war. Similar patterns have also been found by Bwy for Latin America (1968), Hoole, Feierabends (see Feierabends 1966), Tanter (1965, p. 183), and Hibbs (1973, Chpt. 2).

Hazlewood (1973) has analyzed to what extend the factor solutions are stable over time, space, and different techniques. The studies above taken together imply that they are stable over time, while studies made by Borock and Stohl (both quoted in Hazlewood 1973, p. 171) showed that they are not stable if the countries are divided by region or political attributes. Hazlewood's result shows that the factor solutions are stable over time, for different techniques, and for groupings by economic attributes, but they are not stable for centristic or personalistic political systems (Hazlewood 1971, p. 187). This means that the relationships between different forms of disturbances vary depending on the political system in which they occur, which is not very surprising.

The factor analysis done to reduce the number of variables mentioned in Chapter 4 of this study shows how the relationship between the different variables varies from country to country. The factor solutions for six Latin American countries are shown in Appendix E.

From these tables, it is possible to see how different events tend to occur together. In Mexico, riots, deaths in political violence, armed attacks, and protest demonstrations are clustered together. In Brazil, political violence occurs especially during election years and that irregular power transfers are accompanied by negative government sanctions. These factor solutions give a good picture of what happened in these countries from 1948 to 1967. Assuming that the same pattern continued, it should be possible to estimate the chance for a particular event to happen by looking at the other variables in the factor. It should be noted that these factor solutions do not say anything about why these events occur together. Neither do they say anything about the time relationship between the different factors, but more research in this area may be able to tell that.

The conclusion that the relationship between events differs depending on the country is also confirmed by the aforementioned study by Hudson. With data from the *World Handbook* data file, he analyzed how political systems "behave" before, during, and after years of maximum political violence. This he measures by the number of dead in political violence. His results show that the number of different types of events in these years varied very much by region and type of country. Irregular changes were, for example, by far the most common in Latin America, but at the same time the number of protest demonstrations and armed attacks were lowest in this region (Hudson 1971, p. 275). Armed attacks are most common in new nations, while middle-aged nations are characterized by riots, and old nations by protests demonstrations (Hudson 1971, p. 281).

Hudson also found that violent crises and major government changes are relatively independent (Hudson 1971, p. 265). Coups, for example, tend to happen during years with some violence, but there are very often no coups during the year of maximum violence (Hudson 1971, p. 273). The frequency of regular government transfers, on the other hand, increases from the year before the year of maximum violence to the latter year and it continues to increase to the year after.

Hudson could even find a difference in the time sequence of types of events between different types of countries. In newer nations irregular power transfers tend to precede violent crises, while these coincide in older states. Similarly, the level of coups and attempted coups in Asia and the Middle East tend to be higher before the violent peak than in Latin America (Hudson 1971, p. 283).

One example of the theorist group, the Feierabends, has already been discussed above in connection with Green's work. They tried to find a unidimensional scale for all domestic political conflicts (Feierabend 1966; Nesvold 1971a). Our results indicate that different types of events have different relevance to the companies and thus a unidimensional scale is not very useful for political risk evaluation purposes.

Gurr has argued that any measure of political instability must take three things into consideration: participation; the number of people taking part in the disturbing event; the duration of the event; and its intensity, that is, how much it destroyed in lives and material (Gurr 1968, 1104–24). Gurr differs from the empiricists in that he does not count every event as one and from the Feierabends in that he has criteria for how an event is to be classified.

In a later article Gurr makes a division of political instability by building upon the results of the empiricists. He identifies the following three categories:

> *Turmoil.* Relatively spontaneous, unstructured mass strife, including demonstrations, political strikes, riots, political clashes and localized rebellion.
> *Conspiracy.* Intensively organized, relatively small-scale civil strife, including political assassinations, small-scale terrorism, small-scale guerrilla wars, coups, mutinies, and plots and purges, the last two on grounds that they are evidence of planned strife.
> *Internal war.* Large-scale, organized, focussed civil strife, almost always accompanied by extensive violence, including large-scale terrorism and guerilla wars, civil war, private wars and large-scale revolts (Gurr 1971, p. 221).

In a third article, Gurr collapsed Conspiracy and Internal War to Rebellion and, like the empiricists, got two dimensions (Gurr and Durall 1973, p. 143).

Conditions for Political Instability

There is a whole series of theories for explaining political instability, but we will concentrate on two main groups.* The first group is built upon social-psychology theories and the second upon social-structure theories. Feierabends, Gurr, and many others belong to the first group. According to them a country's political stability is decided by the amount of politically relevant agression groups or individuals in the society direct toward each other. "Agression is always the result of frustration," (Feierabends 1966, p. 250) and the degree of frustration is decided by the individual's wants and how well those wants are satisfied. The Feierabends found that if both variables have high values or if both have low, then the frustration is low; but if satisfaction is low while wants formulation is high, this leads to frustration and political instability. They also found that the more rapid change a country experiences, the more unstable it is. (Feierabends 1966, p. 267; Cooper 1974; Hibbs 1973, pp. 160–61, 164, 186, 188). All this is often called the J-curve of rising expectations or relative deprivation. Huntington has stressed the importance of political institutionalization as a stabilizing force for countries experiencing a high degree of social mobilization (Huntington 1968, pp. 55, 79).

---

*Gurr (1973) contains a review of different theories.

Based on this theory Gurr tested the following basic model of civil strife (mass political violence) and obtained a relatively high explanatory value:

$$\text{Magnitude of Political Violence} = \text{RD} + (\text{RD} \times \text{JUST} \times \text{BALANCE}) + \text{E}$$

where RD is the scope and intensity of relative deprivation (discontent) in a population . . . JUST is the scope and intensity of beliefs in that population about the justifiability and utility of engaging in overt strife . . . BALANCE refers to the balance of organization and coercive capabilities between dissident and regime . . . and E is an error term (Gurr and Duval 1973, p. 137).

When operationalizing his variables Gurr has the same problems as have all the researchers doing cross-national analysis based on social psychology. The variables, for example, RD, are theoretically psychological phenomena on the individual level and still the researcher is forced to operationalize these with indicators on the country level. Gurr solved this problem by introducing two intermediate variables on the country level, Strain and Stress. The first is structural characteristics as income distribution, while the second is short-term fluctuations as economic recessions. Doing a cross-sectional analysis, Gurr found Strain to be the most important variable (Gurr and Duval 1973, p. 138). The result may be because of the cross-sectional method used.

As can be seen from Curr's equation above, the degree of repressiveness from the regime is of great importance for political stability. There are many researchers who have found a negative relationship between political instability and coercion (Markus and Nesvold 1972, p. 239ff.; Hibbs 1973, p. 187). This clearly shows one weakness in the definition of political [in]stability in this study. Because only open violence is studied here, a country can be classified as stable although it is potentially very unstable. The question therefore arises whether an act of coercion is to be viewed as stabilizing or unstabilizing. This problem becomes even clearer if a dynamic perspective is taken, and the relationship between earlier coercion and current political stability is examined. Nesvold and Markus then found a curve-linear relationship. "Months which were rated at the midlevel of coerciveness were most likely to be followed by months in which there was high instability" (Markus and Nesvold 1972, p. 240; Hibbs 1973, p. 185). Hibbs describes the vicious circle that can start in this way:

The dominant causal sequence that indirectly relates with dimensions of violence is one in which Protest is met with Repression by elites, which produces in turn an escalated response of Internal War from its recipients. . . . Internal War may then initiate the causal loop that leads to coups, increased repression, more Internal War, and so on (Hibbs 1973, pp. 182, 184, 188; and Gurr and Duval 1973).

Because of the above-mentioned fact that the social psychologists have to use ecological indicators, the differences between them and the social-structuralists are not as great as one might imagine. Jacobson, an example of the latter group, explains political instability by looking at variables outside the political system such as the relationship between support and demand, and internal variables, such as structural complexity, coerciveness, and performance (Jacobson 1973). These can be directly translated to Gurr's terminology, especially at the operational level, where he and Jacobson use the same indicators in principle (Galtung 1971; Parvin 1973).

CONCLUSIONS

This odyssey through the latest findings of some political scientists engaged in research in this area has provided many hints about factors that might be important for an estimation of the probability that a certain event will occur. But it is still not possible to find one coherent theory. Mass political violence can often be explained by the relative deprivation and inequality within a society. To this one must add the utility of using violence, and its costs, which in turn depend on the regime's capability and willingness to engage in coercive variables like tradition, culture, and the institutionalization of the political processes.

There is very little in this research to explain government events, which are most important to the multinational companies. There is little analysis of the relationship between mass political violence and government events besides Hudson's which showed how the time relationship differed from region to region. There are, however, some researchers who have found diffusion effects between countries, especially Latin America (Midlarsky 1970; Li and Thompson 1975).

There is much research to be done in this area. The analyst should probably concentrate on the development over time within countries, rather than engaging in cross-sectional analysis. This study takes a first step in this direction by doing the factor analysis over time. This type of analysis can of course be extended to a number of countries. As has been stated, the causal and time relationships between the factors should then be established, and also, ideally, the events should be tied to the policy of the new government. With this knowledge it would be possible for managers to estimate the political risk.

The validity of the research discussed above and the evidence presented in this study can be found in a study in which nationalization was seen as a function of frustration in the society, in the same way as violence and disturbances were seen above. Knudsen has shown that the degree of frustration, measured in the same way as the Feierabends', and the existence of large foreign interests in a country "explain" a posteriori a big part of the nationalization in Latin America from 1968 to 1971 (Knudsen 1974, pp. 67–68).

This review has limited the discussion to one area of political science; there are many other areas of potentially high relevancy for managers. Especially to be pointed out are the growing theory of voting behavior and other forms of political behavior besides the ones discussed here, the theory on the formation of political issues, and the theories on international regimes such as the international monetary regime.

One problem which has been avoided in the discussion so far, but concerns all kinds of predictions or estimations of events occurring, is the time horizon for which the prediction is made. All the research done and reviewed here is a posteriori and has not been able to deal with the question. But it is a very important issue for the analyst to be aware of when trying to make predictions.

IMPLICATIONS FOR HOST-COUNTRY GOVERNMENTS

Most of what has been said about the bargaining game between corporations and governments is, of course, relevant to the host country governments, especially in the Third World. There are a few points to be made, however. This study has shown how important the image and perceptions of a potential host country are to the investing country. As Root has pointed out, there is much to be gained for the host countries by reducing the gap between image and reality (called the information/confidence gap by Root), since most of the companies' perceptions are based on the worst possible likelihood (Root 1976, p. 9).

Companies tend to consider occurrence of government transfers a natural and important time for change. The period after a government's installation is the time when its international image is created. The government should be aware of this and can even use it to its own advantage. It would be very interesting to see a study comparing the cost of attracting foreign investment by creating a new image or by creating tax incentives. The cost of tax incentives is very high since they work regressively; the higher the profit, the higher the incentive. Perhaps Madison Avenue would be the cheaper alternative. The problem is not a simple one, however, since incentives also have an image-shaping function. The policy towards foreign investors should be as stable, coherent, and clearly stated as possible, and the government should follow it: companies like to know "the rules of the game."

The reaction to transfers and image changes is reinforced by oligopolistic behavior in highly concentrated industries. This can be used by the governments by first attracting one company. Once that company is established, the government's bargaining strength against the other companies in the oligopoly improves tremendously. Again, the old proverb *"divida et impera"* can be applied (Knickerbocker 1972, pp. 196–202).

TABLE A.1

Pearson Correlation between Different Measures of Investment Flows

Country	USᵃ-IMFᵇ	EUᵃ-IMF	US-OECDᶜ	EU-OECD	USOᵈ-US
Mexico	.38	.46	.10	.49	.75
Colombia	−.03	.48	−.35	.11	.51
Venezuela	−.10	−.36	−.28	−.68	.31
Brazil	.66	.36	.29	.77	.10
Chile	−.17	−.15	−.42	−.38	.60
Argentina	−.18	.21	−.51	−.18	.35
France	—ᵉ	—	−.72	.07	.46
Spain	.63	.83	−.09	.06	.84
Italy	.33	−.02	−.57	−.11	.48

[a] The number of manufacturing subsidiaries established by U.S. and European companies respectively as measured in this study (see Chapter 3).

[b] The inflow of (direct investment) capital as measured in this study (see Chapter 3).

[c] The outflow of foreign direct investment from the OECD countries.

[d] The outflow of foreign direct investment as reported by the IMF.

[e] Data not available.

Source; Data compiled by the author from the Harvard Business School's Multinational Enterprise project data bank, the *World Handbook* data file, and the International Monetary Fund, *Balance of Payments Yearbook.*

POLITICAL EVENTS VARIABLES

Renewal of Executive Tenure: an act that reestablishes or reconfirms the term of office of the national executive incumbent leader or ruling group through the country's regular institutionalized channels for this procedure.

Unsuccessful Regular Executive Transfer: an event in which an abortive attempt is made by persons not holding national executive office to obtain such office through legal or conventional procedures.

Unsuccessful Irregular Power Transfer: a reported attempt by an organized group to remove and replace the incumbent national executive outside the conventional procedures for transferring formal power.

Irregular Power Transfer: a change in the office of national executive from one leader or ruling group to another. The change is accomplished outside the conventional legal or customary procedures for transferring power in effect at the time of the event. Such events are accompanied either by actual physical violence or with the clear threat of violence.

Regular Executive Transfer: a change in the office of national executive from one leader or ruling group to another that is accomplished through conventional legal or customary procedures and is accompanied by actual or directly threatened physical violence.

Election: an act of collective choice-making by a body of people entitled to vote.

Protest Demonstration: a nonviolent gathering of people organized for the announced purpose of protesting against a regime, government, or one or more of its leaders, or against its ideology, policy, intended policy, or lack of policy, or against its previous action or intended action.

Regime-Support Demonstration: an organized nonviolent gathering of people whose purpose is to lend support to a government.

Political Strike: a work stoppage by a body of industrial or service workers or a stoppage of normal academic life by students to protest against a regime, a government, government leaders, a government's policy or action.

Riot: a violent demonstration or disturbance involving a large number of people.

Armed Attack: an act of political conflict carried out by (or on behalf of) an organized group with the object of weakening or destroying the power exercised by another organized group. It is characterized by bloodshed, physical struggle, or the destruction of property. . . . The category is intended to encompass all organized political violence in a political system, and it is intended to exclude all non-violent protest and incidents of turmoil.

Political Assassination: politically motivated murder or attempted murder of a high government official or politician.

Death from Political Violence: a body count. The deaths reported occur mainly in conjunction with armed attacks, but also with riots and to a lesser extent with demonstrations.

Governmental Sanction: an action taken by the authorities to neutralize, suppress or eliminate a perceived threat to the security of the government, the regime or the state itself.

Political Execution: an event in which a person or group of persons is put to death under orders of the national authorities while in the custody of those authorities.

Relaxation of Government Restriction on Political Activity: an event in which a government modifies or eliminates restrictions on political action or expression of the type classified as government sanctions.

Source: *World Handbook of Political and Social Indicators,* (Ann Arbor: Inter-university Consortium for Political Research, 1971), Codebook sections II–IV: Events.

APPENDIX C

TABLE C.1

Classification of Industries

		Classification		
SIC[a] Code	Industry	Large-Scale	Low Labor-Intensity	High-Concentration Ratio
200	Food N.S.F.[b]			
201	Meat products			
202	Dairy products		x	
203	Canned foods			
204	Grain mill products		x	
205	Bakery products			
206	Sugar	x	x	x
207	Confectionery			
208	Beverages		x	
209	Miscellaneous food products		x	
211	Cigarettes	x	x	x
212	Cigars			x
213	Tobacco		x	x
214	Tobacco stemming			
220	Textiles N.S.F.			
221	Woven cotton	x		
222	Woven man-made fiber and silk			
223	Woven wool			
224	Narrow fabrics			
225	Knitting mills			
226	Dyeing			
227	Floor covering			
228	Yarn and thread			
229	Miscellaneous textile goods			
230	Clothing N.S.F.			
231	Men's suits, coats			
232	Men's allied garments			
233	Women's outerwear			
234	Women's children's under garments			
235	Hats			
236	Girls' outerwear			
237	Fur goods			

SIC[a] Code	Industry	Large-Scale	Low Labor-Intensity	High-Concentration Ratio
			Classification	
238	Miscellaneous apparel			
239	Miscellaneous fabricated textiles			
240	Lumber and wood N.S.F.			
241	Logging			
242	Sawmills			
243	Wood products			
244	Wooden containers			
249	Miscellaneous wood products			
250	Furniture N.S.F.			
251	Household furniture			
252	Office furniture			
253	Public building furniture			
254	Office and store fixtures			
259	Miscellaneous furniture and fixtures			
260	Paper N.S.F.			
261	Pulp mills		x	
262	Paper mills	x		
263	Paperboard mills	x	x	
264	Paper products			
265	Paperboard containers			
266	Building paper			
271	Newspapers		x	
272	Periodicals			
273	Books		x	
274	Miscellaneous publishing		x	
275	Commercial printing			
276	Business forms			
277	Greeting cards			x
278	Blankbooks and bookbinding			
279	Service for printing			
280	Chemicals N.S.F.			
281	Industrial chemicals	x	x	
282	Plastics	x	x	x
283	Drugs		x	
284	Soap, cosmetics		x	
285	Paints		x	
286	Wood chemicals			x
287	Agricultural chemicals		x	
289	Miscellaneous chemicals		x	
290	Petroleum N.S.F			

(continued)

TABLE C.1 (continued)

SIC[a] Code	Industry	Large-Scale	Low Labor-Intensity	High-Concentration Ratio
291	Petroleum refining	x	x	
295	Paving and roofing			
299	Miscellaneous petroleum and coal		x	
300	Rubber N.S.F.			
301	Tires	x	x	x
302	Rubber footwear	x		x
303	Reclaimed rubber			x
306	Fabricated rubber, N.E.C.[c]			
307	Miscellaneous plastics			
310	Leather N.S.F.			
311	Leather tanning			
312	Leather packing			x
313	Shoe cut stock			
314	Footwear			
315	Leather gloves			
316	Luggage			
317	Handbags			
319	Leather goods, N.E.C.			
320	Stone, glass, etc. N.S.F.			
321	Flat glass	x		x
322	Glassware	x		x
323	Purchased glass			
324	Cement	x	x	
325	Structural clay products			
326	Pottery			
327	Concrete, gypsum, and plaster			
328	Cut stone			
329	Miscellaneous nonmetallic minerals			
331	Steel works	x		
332	Iron and steel foundries			
333	Primary smelting nonferrous metals	x	x	x
334	Secondary smelting nonferrous metals			
335	Rolling nonferrous metals	x		
336	Nonferrous foundries			
339	Miscellaneous primary metals			
340	Fabricated metal N.S.F.			
341	Metal cans	x		x
342	General hardware			

SIC[a] Code	Industry	Large-Scale	Low Labor-Intensity	High-Concentration Ratio
		Classification		
343	Heating and plumbing			
344	Structural metal products			
345	Screws			
346	Metal stampings			
347	Coating, engraving			
348	Miscellaneous fabricated wire			
349	Miscellaneous fabricated metal			
350	Nonelectrical machinery N.S.F.			
351	Engines and turbines	x		x
352	Farm machinery			
353	Construction machinery			
354	Metalworking machinery			
355	Special industry machinery			
356	General industrial machinery			
357	Office machines	x		x
358	Service industry machines			
359	Miscellaneous machinery			
361	Electric transmission equipment			
362	Electrical industrial apparatus			
363	Household appliances			x
364	Electric lighting			
365	Radio and television sets			
366	Communication equipment	x		
367	Electronic components			
369	Miscellaneous electrical machinery			x
371	Motor vehicles	x	x	x
372	Aircraft	x		
373	Ships			
374	Railroad	x		x
375	Motorcycles, bicycles			x
379	Miscellaneous transportation equipment			
381	Engineering and scientific instruments			
382	Instruments for measuring			
383	Optical instruments			
384	Medical instruments and supplies			
385	Ophthalmic goods			
386	Photographic equipment			x

(continued)

TABLE C.1   (continued)

SIC[a] Code	Industry	Classification		
		Large-Scale	Low Labor-Intensity	High-Concentration Ratio
387	Watches, clocks			
391	Jewelry			
393	Musical instruments			
394	Toys			
395	Pens, pencils			
396	Costume jewelry			
399	Miscellaneous manufacturing industries			

[a] Standard Industrial Classification.
[b] Not specified further.
[c] Not elsewhere classified.

Sources: Scale and Labor Intensity was computed from: U.S. Department of Commerce, Bureau of the Census, Census of Manufacturers, Survey and Subject Statistics 1963 (Washington, D.C.: U.S. Government Printing Office, 1966), Table 3, pp. 46 ff. Concentration ratio was computed from: U.S. Congress, Senate Subcommittee on Anti-Trust and Monopoly of the Commission on the Judiciary, *Concentration Ratios in Manufacturing Industries 1963*, 89th Congress, 2nd Session, 1966.

STEP-WISE REGRESSION EQUATIONS

Regression Analysis

In order to see if any country-specific conclusions could be made or if the historical pattern of what has happened in the countries included in this study could be described, step-wise regression analysis was done for each country. The dependent variables were the total number of subsidiaries established by U.S. and by European companies over time. The independent variables were

TABLE D.1

Step-wise Regression Equations for Latin America

Dependent Variable	Time Lag	Independent Variables	beta	F
Mexico				
U.S. companies $R^2 = .21$; $N = 19$	0	unsuccessful executive transfer	.46	4.61
Colombia				
U.S. companies $R^2 = .48$; $N = 18$	2	unsuccessful irregular transfer	.69	14.56
Venezuela				
U.S. companies $R^2 = .43$; $N = 18$ $F = 5.64$		unsuccessful executive transfer renewals of power	.50 .46	6.64 5.49
Brazil				
U.S. companies $R^2 = .43$; $N = 19$ $F = 6.08$	1	unsuccessful executive transfer regular executive transfer	−.61 .45	9.85 5.46
U.S. companies $R^2 = .42$; $N = 18$ $F = 5.40$	2	irregular power transfer regular executive transfer	.51 −.41	6.67 4.44*
European companies $R^2 = .23$; $N = 19$	1	irregular power transfer	.47	4.97
Chile				
U.S. companies $R^2 = .31$; $N = 18$	2	deaths in political violence	.56	7.29
Argentina				
European companies $R^2 = .29$; $N = 19$	1	regular executive transfer	.54	6.87

* All others significant at the 5 percent level.
Source: Compiled by the author.

TABLE D.2

Step-wise Regression Equations for Europe and Africa

Dependent Variable	Time Lag	Independent Variables	beta	F
France				
U.S. companies	1	unsuccessful irregular transfer	−.46	4.44*
$R^2 = .21$; N = 19				
U.S. companies	2	irregular power transfer	.56	7.70
$R^2 = .41$; N = 18		negative sanctions	−.42	4.41*
F = 5.29				
European companies	2	deaths	.82	33.05
$R^2 = .82$; N = 18				
Spain				
U.S. companies	2	negative sanctions	−.58	8.42
$R^2 = .34$; N = 18				
Italy				
U.S. companies	2	unsuccessful executive transfer	.47	4.63
$R^2 = .22$; N = 18				
European companies	1	unsuccessful executive transfer	.49	5.47
$R^2 = .24$; N = 19				
South Africa				
U.S. companies	2	regular executive transfer	.47	4.43*
$R^2 = .22$; N = 18				
European companies	2	regular executive transfer	.50	5.44
$R^2 = .25$; N = 18				
Nigeria				
European companies	1	unsuccessful irregular	.54	6.94
$R^2 = .29$; N = 19				

*All others significant at the 5 percent level.
Source: Compiled by the author.

deaths in political violence (natural logarithm), negative (natural logarithm) sanctions and some of the government event variables. The dependent variables were lagged 0, 1, and 2 years.

The significant equations can be seen in Tables D. 1, D. 2, and D. 3. It is very hard to see any pattern in the tables. Of the 66 possible equations, 17 are significant at the 5 percent level. It is to be noted, however, that the countries are not drawn from a random sample, which means that significance cannot be spoken of in the strict sense of the word. Equations with no time lag are significant only in two of these 17 cases. This shows that there is some validity in the results, since without time-lag equations should have been significant as often as the ones with a time lag if the correlation were caused by random factors. Further, most of the variables entered into the equations are government disturbances.

TABLE D.3

Step-wise Regression Equations for Asia

Dependent Variable	Time Lag	Independent Variables	beta	F
India				
U.S. companies $R^2 = .22; N = 19$	0	regular executive transfer	−.45	4.23[*]
European companies $R^2 = .27; N = 18$ F = 11.48	2	renewals of power deaths in political violence	−.70 .60	17.20 12.53
Pakistan				
European companies $R^2 = .18; N = 19$	1	irregular power transfer	−.43	3.90[*]
Philippines				
U.S. companies $R^2 = .21; N = 19$	1	regular executive transfer	.46	4.64

[*] All others significant at the 5 percent level.
Source: Compiled by the author.

APPENDIX E

TABLE E.1

Factor Solutions for Latin America

Variable	F1	F2	F3	F4	F5	H^2
			Factors			
Regime support demonstrations	.903	−.001	.112	−.163	.083	.861
Unsuccessful executive transfers	.910	−.010	−.107	−.038	−.045	.844
Unsuccessful irregular power transfers	.835	−.177	.456	.031	−.027	.938
Political assassinations	.038	.790	−.020	−.103	−.049	.640
Political strikes	−.213	.714	.012	.120	.171	.599
Acts of negative sanction	.074	.757	.508	.051	−.028	.841
Riots	.105	.416	.802	.094	.014	.837
Deaths political violence	.149	−.156	.841	.094	.014	.837
Armed attacks	.349	.182	.587	−.075	.206	.548
Protest demonstrations	−.074	.024	.702	−.171	.061	.531
Elections	−.122	−.023	.401	.765	−.360	.891
Executive adjustments	−.019	−.217	−.250	.768	.207	.742
Regular executive transfers	−.127	.413	.046	.819	.149	.882
Relaxation of sanctions	−.070	−.043	.070	.318	.614	.490
External interventions	−.085	−.118	−.144	.133	−.829	.747
Percent common variance explained	33.1	25.5	17.6	12.6	11.2	100.0
Percent total variance explained	24.8	19.1	13.2	9.4	8.4	74.9

Notes: Principal component using Kaiser's criteria for deciding the number of factors and varimax rotation. The same method used for all countries. Values for the unrotated factors are used since the explanatory values of rotated factors are only a function of the number of variables loading high on that factor (Nie, Bent, and Hull 1970, p. 217).

In this analysis two more variables are added to the original list of independent variables (Chapter 3 and Appendix B). Since this analysis was done before it was decided to eliminate these variables from the main analysis. The variables are: *Executive adjustment,* a modification in the membership of a national executive body that does not signify a transfer of formal power from one leader or ruling group to another. *External intervention,* an attempt by an actor to engage in military activity within the target country with the intent of influencing the authority structure of that country.

Source: World Handbook of Political and Social Indicators, (Ann Arbor: Inter-university Consortium for Political Research, 1971), Codebook sections II–IV: Events.

TABLE E.2

Factor Solutions for Colombia

Variable	Factors					
	F1	F2	F3	F4	F5	H²
Regime support demonstrations	.865	.242	-.011	-.176	.125	.854
Political strikes	.947	.138	.099	-.066	.018	.931
Unsuccessful irregular power transfers	.917	.133	.197	.011	.078	.904
Protest demonstrations	.261	.833	-.197	-.013	-.147	.823
Renewals of power	.265	.898	-.023	.062	-.049	.884
Irregular power transfers	.014	.841	.417	-.034	.064	.887
Executive adjustments	-.326	.011	-.514	.225	.220	.470
Regular executive transfers	.016	-.167	.672	.316	.420	.756
Relaxation of political sanctions	.207	.471	.785	.058	.091	.893
Riots	-.102	.208	.122	.871	.065	.831
Deaths political violence	-.126	-.212	-.009	.819	-.084	.738
Armed attacks	.040	.099	-.466	.511	.033	.491
Political assassinations	.034	-.045	-.001	.019	-.673	.456
Elections	.187	.038	.289	.144	.668	.586
Acts of negative sanction	.109	.397	.236	.195	-.739	.810
Percent common variance explained	36.5	20.6	19.1	13.4	10.4	100.0
Percent total variance explained	27.5	15.5	14.4	10.1	7.9	75.4

Source: World Handbook of Political and Social Indicators. (Ann Arbor: Inter-university Consortium for Political Research, 1971), Codebook sections II-IV: Events.

TABLE E.3

Factor Solutions for Venezuela

Variable*			Factors				H²
	F1	F2	F3	F4	F5	F6	
Riots	.692	.559	.033	.069	.270	.041	.872
Deaths political violence	.900	-.072	.098	.064	.162	-.032	.856
Political strikes	.721	.108	.167	.564	-.020	.063	.882
Unsuccessful irregular power transfers	.666	.561	-.111	.162	.275	.070	.878
Executive adjustments	.634	.089	.281	-.101	.412	-.028	.670
Relaxation of sanctions	.921	.026	.098	-.076	-.023	-.176	.896
Regime support demonstrations	.095	.877	-.008	.189	-.089	-.019	.817
Negative sanctions	.240	.840	.310	.134	.052	-.013	.879
External interventions	-.130	.860	-.023	-.149	-.105	-.107	.802
Armed attacks	.212	.075	.919	.058	-.056	-.066	.907
Protest demonstrations	.177	.440	-.098	.761	.175	-.057	.847
Regular executive transfers	.438	.305	-.228	-.572	.295	.081	.757
Political assassinations	.025	.356	.490	-.323	.518	-.270	.813
Elections	.134	-.115	.471	.153	.678	.378	.879
Irregular power transfers	.241	-.108	-.203	.018	.855	-.109	.854
Renewals of power	-.135	-.080	-.078	-.055	-.031	.961	.958
Percent common variance explained	41.4	19.0	11.9	11.0	9.4	7.4	100.0
Percent total variance explained	35.1	16.1	10.1	9.3	8.0	6.3	84.8

*Unsuccessful regular executive transfers not included because factor scores were then indeterminate.

Source: World Handbook of Political and Social Indicators, (Ann Arbor: Inter-university Consortium for Political Research, 1971), Codebook sections II–IV: Events.

TABLE E.4

Factor Solutions for Argentina

Variable*	Factors					H²
	F1	F2	F3	F4	F5	
Deaths political violence	.932	.145	.038	-.015	.159	.917
Political assassinations	.779	-.023	.025	.128	-.073	.630
Armed attacks	.620	.576	.105	-.119	.363	.873
Protest demonstrations	.765	.494	.137	.096	.107	.868
Irregular power transfers	.581	.650	-.121	.262	.027	.844
Acts of negative sanction	.903	.157	.112	-.045	.114	.868
Acts of relaxation of sanctions	.786	-.125	.189	-.003	-.109	.681
Political strikes	.018	.747	.215	-.036	-.149	.628
Executive adjustments	.031	.833	-.013	-.245	.189	.791
Regular executive transfers	.045	.540	.300	.605	-.043	.751
Regime support demonstrations	.228	.014	.898	.026	.103	.870
Executions	-.085	.081	.922	-.009	-.008	.864
Elections	-.235	-.174	-.256	.559	.444	.660
Renewals of power	-.127	.200	-.207	-.793	-.090	.736
Unsuccessful irregular power transfers	.222	.131	.149	.168	.799	.756
Riots	.438	.439	.077	.435	-.492	.822
Percent common variance explained	45.0	17.3	15.2	12.4	10.3	100.0
Percent total variance explained	35.3	13.6	11.9	9.7	8.1	78.5

*Unsuccessful regular executive transfers not included because factor scores were then indeterminate.

Source: World Handbook of Political and Social Indicators. (Ann Arbor: Inter-university Consortium for Political Research, 1971), Codebook sections II–IV: Events.

TABLE E.5

Factor Solutions for Chile

Variable	Factors						
	F1	F2	F3	F4	F5	F6	H²
Riots	.875	-.193	.249	.146	.066	-.038	.892
Deaths political violence	.814	-.056	-.195	.106	-.103	-.008	.726
Relaxation of sanctions	.803	.198	.185	-.266	.083	.293	.881
Renewals of power	-.015	.904	-.213	.005	.027	-.001	.863
Executive adjustments	-.090	.883	.118	-.047	-.067	.025	.809
Elections	.334	-.174	.723	.314	-.172	.015	.793
Regime executive transfers	-.081	-.001	.885	-.130	-.055	.051	.812
Regime support demonstrations	-.186	-.148	.213	.872	.035	-.020	.863
Political strikes	-.295	-.136	-.372	-.051	-.577	.429	.764
Unsuccessful irregular political transfers	-.173	-.161	-.206	-.071	.824	-.002	.783
Acts of negative sanction	.307	.459	-.172	-.085	.589	.451	.893
Armed attacks	.094	.022	.090	.018	-.019	.935	.893
Percent common variance explained	25.9	22.6	14.9	14.2	12.4	10.1	100.0
Percent total variance explained	21.6	18.8	12.4	11.8	10.3	8.4	83.3

Source: World Handbook of Political and Social Indicators, (Ann Arbor: Inter-university Consortium for Political Research, 1971), Codebook sections II–IV: Events.

TABLE E.6
Factor Solutions for Brazil

Variable	F1	F2	F3	F4	H²
Political assassinations	.910	-.116	.194	.174	.909
Political strikes	.779	.091	-.068	.195	.657
Renewals of power	.812	-.060	.084	.049	.673
Regular executive transfers	.773	.122	-.251	.434	.818
Executions/unsuccessful regular executive transfers	.960	-.114	.092	-.144	.963
Irregular power transfers	-.040	.779	-.052	-.224	.661
Executive adjustments	.019	.899	-.117	.062	.882
Acts of negative sanction	-.000	.804	.199	.284	.766
Relaxation of sanctions	-.080	.882	.165	.021	.812
Riots	-.010	.106	.821	.060	.689
Deaths political violence	.259	-.187	.702	-.064	.598
Armed attacks	.407	.299	.682	-.125	.735
Elections	-.264	.039	.754	-.011	.641
Protest demonstrations	-.016	-.276	.312	.842	.883
Regime support demonstrations	.110	.420	-.214	.780	.844
Percent common variance explained	34.9	29.4	21.6	14.1	100.0
Percent total variance explained	26.7	22.5	16.5	10.8	76.5

Source: *World Handbook of Political and Social Indicators,* (Ann Arbor: Inter-university Consortium for Political Research, 1971), Codebook sections II-IV: Events.

127

REFERENCES

van Agtmael, Antoine W. 1976. "Evaluating the risk of lending to developing countries." *Euromoney,* April.

Aharoni, Y. 1966. *The Foreign Investment Decisions Process.* Cambridge: Harvard University Press.

Ake, Claude. 1975. "A Definition of Political Stability." *Comparative Politics,* January.

Allison, Graham I. 1971. *Essence of Decision: Explaining the Cuban Missile Crisis.* Boston: Little Brown.

Allison, Graham I., and Halperin, M. 1972. "Bureaucratic Politics: A Paradigm and Some Policy Implications." In *Theory and Policy in International Relations,* ed. R. Tanter and R. H. Ullman, Princeton: Princeton University Press.

Ayres, Robert L. 1975. "Political Regimes, Explanatory Variables and Public Policy in Latin America." *The Journal of Developing Areas,* October.

Balance of Payments Yearbook. 1954–1972. Washington, D.C.: The International Monetary Fund.

Bauer, Raymond A., de Sola Pool, Ithiel, and Dexter, Lewis Anthony. 1963. *American Business and Public Policy.* New York: Atherton.

Behrman, Jack N. 1974a. *Decision Criteria for Foreign Direct Investment in Latin America.* New York: Council of Americas.

———. 1974b. *Conflicting Constraints on the Multinational Enterprise: Potential Resolution.* New York: Council of Americas.

Bennet, Peter D., and Green, Robert T. 1972. "Political Instability as a Determinant of Direct Foreign Investment in Marketing." *Journal of Marketing Research,"* May.

Berggvist, A., and Leander, B. 1970. *Etablering av Producerande Dotter Bolag Utomlands.* Lund: Studentlitteratur.

Boddewyn, Jean, Cracco, Etienne F. 1972. "The Political Game in World Business." *Columbia Journal of World Business,* January-February.

Borock, C. M. 1967. Universal and Regional Dimensions of Domestic Conflict. PhD. dissertation, University of Cincinnati.

Bower, Joseph L. 1970. *Managing the Resource Allocation Process,* Harvard Graduate School of Business, Division of Research, Boston.

Brook, M. S., and Remmers, H. L. 1971. *The Strategy of Multinational Enterprise.* Bristol, England: Longman.

Bureau of the Budget, Office of Statistical Standards. 1967. *Standard Classification Manual 1967.* Washington, D.C.: U.S. Government Printing Office.

Burgess, Philip M., and Lawton, Raymond W. 1972. *Indicators of International Behavior: An Assessment of Events Data Research.* International Studies Series, vol. 1, Beverly Hills: Sage.

Business International. 1968. "Evaluating Projects Abroad." Management monograph.

Business International. 1969. "Rating Environmental Risks in Foreign Investments." Management monograph.

Business International. 1970. "Nationalism in Latin America. Management monograph.

Business International. 1975. "Briefing Memorandum, World Forecasting Roundtable, 1976–78." Confidential mimeograph.

Bwy, D. P. 1968. "Political Instability in Latin America: The Cross Cultural Test of A Causal Model." *Latin American Research Review,* Spring.

Carlsson, S. 1969. *International Financial Decisions.* Upsala: Laromedelsforlagen.

Cooper, Mark H. 1974. "A Reinterpretation of the Causes of Turmoil: The Effects of Culture and Modernity." *Comparative Political Studies,* October.

Cyert, Richard M., and March, James G. 1963. *A Behavioral Theory of the Firm.* Englewood Cliffs: Prentice-Hall.

Davies, Otto A.; Dempster, M. A. H.; and Wildavsky, Aaron. 1966. "A Theory of the Budgetary Process," *American Political Science Review,* September, pp. 529–47.

Drew, Paul. 1974. "Domestic Political Violence: Some Problems of Measurement." *The Sociological Review,* February.

Dunning, John. H. ed. 1974. *Economic Analysis and the Multinational Enterprise.* London: Allen and Unwin.

Easton, David E. 1965. *A System Analysis of Political Life.* New York: John Wiley.

Eckstein, Harry. 1971. *The Evaluation of Political Performance: Problems and Dimensions.* Comparative Political Series, vol. 2. London: Sage.

Feierabend, Ivo K.; Feierabend, Rosalind L.; and Nesvold, Betty D. 1973. "The Comparative Study of Revolution and Violence." *Comparative Politics,* April.

Fortune. 1968. Sept. 15.

Galtung, Johann. 1971. "A Structural Theory of Imperialism." *Journal of Peace Research,* no. 2, pp. 81–118.

Goodsell, Charles T. 1974. *American Corporations and Peruvian Politics.* Cambridge: Harvard University Press.

Green, Robert T. 1972. *Political Instability as a Determinant of U.S. Foreign Investment.* Studies in Marketing, no. 17, Bureau of Business Research, Graduate School of Business, University of Texas, Auston.

————. 1974b. "Political Structures as a Predictor of Radical Political Change." *Columbia Journal of World Business,* Spring.

Green, Robert T. and Korth, Christopher M. 1974a. "Political Instability and the Foreign Investor." *California Management Review,* Fall.

Groo, E. S. 1971. "Choosing Foreign Locations: One Company's Experience." *Columbia Journal of World Business,* September/October.

Gurr, Ted Robert. 1968. "A Causal Model of Civil Strife: A Comparative Analysis Using New Indices." *The American Political Science Review,* December, pp. 1104–24.

————. 1973. "The Revolution-Social-Change Nexus: Some Old Theories and New Hypotheses." *Comparative Politics,* April.

————. 1974. "Persistence and Change in Political Systems, 1800–1971." *American Political Science Review,* December, pp: 1482–1504.

Gurr, Ted Robert, and McClelland, Muriel. 1971. *Political Performance: A Twelve-Nation Study.* Comparative Political Series, vol. 2. London: Sage.

Gurr, Ted Robert and Duvall, Raymond. 1973. *Comparative Political Studies,* July.

Haarkoff, Frank E. 1970. "Don't Let Your Wife Pick Plant Site Abroad." *Marketing Insight.* February 4.

Haendel, Dan, and West, Gerald T. with Meadow, Robert G. 1975. *Overseas Investment and Political Risk.* Foreign Policy Research Institute Monograph Series, no. 21, Philadelphia.

Hayes, Richard D. 1971. "An Introspective Structure for Foreign Investment Decisions." *MSU Business Topics* 19, October.

Hazlewood, Leo A. 1973. "Concept and Measurement Stability in the Study of Conflict Behavior Within Nations." *Comparative Political Studies,* July.

Hibbs, Douglas A. 1973. *Mass Political Violence: A Cross-National Analysis* New York: John Wiley.

Hoole, Francis W. 1964. Political Stability and Instability Within Nations: Masters thesis, San Diego State College.

Hörnell, E.; Vahlne J.-E.; and Wiedersheim-Paul I. 1973.

Hoskins, William R. 1970. "How to Counter Expropriations." *Harvard Business Review,* September/October.

Hudson, Michael C. 1971. "Political Protest and Power Transfers in Crisis Periods, Regional Structural and Environmental Comparisons." *Comparative Political Studies,* October.

Huntington, Samuel. 1968. *Political Order in Changing Societies.* New Haven: Yale University Press.

Hurwitz, Leon. 1973. "Contemporary Approaches to Political Stability." *Comparative Politics,* April.

Hymer, Stephen. 1976. *"The International Operations of National Firms: A Study of Direct Foreign Investment,* Cambridge: M.I.T. Press.

Jacobson, Alvin L. 1973. "Intrasocietal Conflict: A Preliminary Text of a Structural-Level Theory." *Comparative Political Studies,* April.

Kantor, Harry 1969. *Patterns of Politics and Political Systems in Latin America.* New York: Rand McNally.

Keegan, Warren J. 1974. "Multinational Scanning," *Administrative Science Quarterly,* September.

Keohane, Robert O., and Van Doorn, Ooms. 1975. "The Multinational Firm and International Regulation." *International Organization,* Winter.

Knickerbocker, Fredrick T. 1973. *Oligopolistic Reaction and Multinational Enterprise.* Cambridge: Harvard University Press.

Knudsen, Harald. 1974. "Explaining the National Propensity to Expropriate: An Ecological Approach." *Journal of International Business Studies,* Fall.

Kobrin, Stephen J. 1975. The Environmental Determinants of Foreign Direct Investment: An Ex Post Empirical Analysis." Working Paper, Alfred P. Sloan School of Management, M.I.T.

Lehtinen, Dexter W. 1974. "Modernization, Political Development and Stability." *Stanford Journal of International Studies,* Spring, pp. 219–45.

Li, Richar P. Y., and Thompson, William R. 1975. "The 'Coup Contagion' Hypothesis." *Journal of Conflict Resolution,* March.

Liander, Bertil; Terpstra, Vern; Yochino, Michael; and Sherbini, A. A. 1967. *Comparative Analysis for International Marketing.* Boston: Allyn and Bacon.

Lipson, Charles H. 1976. "Corporate Preferences and Public Policies: Foreign Aid Sanctions and Investment Protection." *World Politics,* vol. XXVIII, no. 3, April.

Litvak, I. A. and Maule, C. T. eds. 1970. *Foreign Investment: The Experience of Host Countries.* New York: Praeger.

Marcus, Gregory B., and Nesvold, Betty A. 1972. "Governmental Coerciveness and Political Instability: An Exploratory Study of Cross-National Patterns." *Comparative Political Studies,* July.

Midlarsky, Manus. 1970. "Mathematical Models of Instability and a Theory of Diffusion." *International Studies Quarterly,* March.

Miller, Robert R., and Weigel, Dale. 1972. "The Motivation for Foreign Direct Investment." *Journal of International Business,* Fall.

Moran, Theodore H. 1973. "Transnational Strategies of Protection and Defense by Multinational Corporations: Spreading the Risk and Raising the Cost for Nationalization in Natural Resources." *International Organization,* Spring.

Morrison, Donald G., and Stevenson, Hugh Michael. 1974. "Measuring Social and Political Requirements for System Stability: Empirical Validation of an Index Using Latin American and African Data." *Comparative Political Studies,* July.

Murray, J. Alex. 1972. "Intelligence Systems of the MNC's." *Columbia Journal of World Business,* September/October.

National Industrial Conference Board: Obstacles and Incentives to Private Foreign Investment, 1967–68. 1969. Vol. 1: Obstacles. New York: National Industrial Conference Board.

Nehrt, Lee C. 1970. *The Political Climate for Private Foreign Investment.* New York: Praeger.

Nesvold, Betty A. 1969. "Scalogram Analysis of Political Violence." *Comparative Political Studies,* July.

Nie, N. H.; Bent, D. H.; and Hull, C. H. 1970. *Statistical Package for the Social Sciences.* New York: McGraw-Hill.

Nye, Joseph S., Jr. 1974. "Multinational Corporations in World Politics." *Foreign Affairs,* October.

Organization for Economic Cooperation and Development. 1967. *The Flow of Direct Investment to the Less Developed Countries, 1961–1965,* Paris.

————. 1968. "The Climate for Private Investment in Developing Countries," Working Document, DAC (68) 24, BIAC Secretariat, Paris.

————. 1972. "The Relation of Expropriatory Action by Developing Countries to Foreign Private Investment Flows," Development Centre Research Division. Mimeographed. CD/R/72:5. Paris.

Parvin, Manoucher. 1973. "Economic Determinants of Political Unrest." *Journal of Conflict Resolution,* June.

Phatak, A. V. 1974. *Managing Multinational Corporations.* New York: Praeger.

Piper, J. R. 1971. "How U.S. Firms Evaluate Foreign Investment Opportunities." *MSU Business Topics,* Summer.

Pollock, David, and Ritter, Arch R. M., 1973. *Latin American Prospects for the 1970's: What Kind of Revolutions.* New York: Praeger.

Prahalad, C. K. 1976. "Strategic Choices in Diversified MNCs." *Harvard Business Review,* July/August.

Prayor, Fredrick L. 1972. "An International Comparison of Concentration Ratios." *Review of Economics and Statistics,* May.

Regezzi, G. 1973. "Theories of the Determinants of Direct Foreign Investment." *IMF Staff Papers,* July.

Reuber, Grant L., with Crookell, Emerson M. and Gallais-Hamonno, G. 1973. *Private Foreign Investment in Development.* Oxford: Clarendon Press.

Richardson, J. D. 1971. "On Going Abroad." *The Quarterly Review of Economics and Business,* Winter.

Robinson, R. D. 1964. *International Business Policy.* New York: Holt Rinehart, and Winston.

Robock, Stepan H. 1971. "Political Risk: Identification and Assessment." *Columbia Journal of World Business,* July/August.

Rothberg, B. G. 1975. "A Decision Theoretical Model of Eastern Hemisphere Oil Exploration." DBA thesis. Graduate School of Business Administration, Harvard University, Boston.

Root, Franklin R. 1968. "U.S. Business Abroad and the Political Risks." *MSU Business Topics,* Winter.

————. 1972. "Analyzing Political Risk in International Business." In *Multinational Enterprise in Transition: Selected Readings and Essays* eds. A. Kapoor and Phillip Grub. Detroit: Darwin Press.

————. 1976. "The Management by LDC Governments of the Political Risk Trade-off in Direct Foreign Investment." Paper presented to the International Studies Association, Toronto, February 1976.

Rosen, Steven J. 1974. "The Open Door Imperative and U.S. Foreign Policy." In *Testing Theories of Economic Imperialism.* eds. Steven J. Rosen and James R. Kurth., Lexington: Lexington Books.

Rummel, R. J. 1963. "Dimensions of Conflict Behavior within and between Nations." *General Systems Yearbook* 8:1–50.

————. 1965. "A Field Theory of Social Action with Application to Conflict within Nations." *General Systems Yearbook* 10:183–211.

————. 1966. "Dimensions of Conflict Behavior within Nations, 1946–59." *Journal of Conflict Resolution,* March.

Sampson, S. 1973. *The Sovereign State of ITT.* New York: Stein and Day.

Shetty, K. 1970. "Evaluating Foreign Investment Opportunities." *Economic and Business Bulletin,* Fall.

Sjostedt, Gunnar. 1974. "Integration and 'Actor Capability,' a survey of the theories of regional, political integration." Research Report. Stockholm: The Swedish Institute of International Affairs.

Stevens, Guy V. G. 1969. "U.S. Direct Manufacturing Investment to Latin America: Some Economic and Political Determinants." AID Research Paper. Mimeographed.

Stobaugh, Robert B. 1969a. "Where in the World Should We Put That Plant?" *Harvard Business Review,* January/February.

————. 1969b. "How to Analyze Foreign Investment Climate." *Harvard Business Review,* September/October.

Stohl, M. 1971. The Study of Conflict Behavior Within and Between Nations: Some New Evidence. Paper presented at the Midwest Political Science Association Meetings, Chicago.

Stopford, John M., and Wells, Louis T., Jr. 1972. *Managing the Multinational Enterprise: Organizing of the Firm and Ownership of the Subsidiaries.* New York: Basic Books.

Stonehill, A., and Nathansson, L. 1968. "Capital Budgeting and the Multinational Corporation." *California Management Review,* Summer.

Sullivan, Laurance K. 1974. "Economic Correlates of Political Violence." *Stanford Journal of International Studies,* Spring, pp. 198–218.

Svedberg, Peter. 1972. *Utländska Privata Investeringar i Underutvecklade Länder,* Promemoria Di SOU :90 Stockholm: Utrikesdepartementet.

Swansbrough, Robert H. 1972. "The American Investor's View of Latin American Economic Nationalism." *Inter-American Economic Affairs,* Winter.

Tanter, R. 1965. "Dimensions of Conflict Behavior within Nations, 1955–1960: Turmoil and Internal War." *Peace Research Society (International) Papers,* no. 3.

————. 1966. "Dimensions of Conflict Behavior within and between Nations, 1958–1968," *Journal of Conflict Resolution,* March.

Tiffany, K. C. 1968. "Decisive Factors in the Decision to Invest in One Country Rather Than Another." *Canadian Chartered Accountant,* 96, March.

Truitt, J. Frederick. 1970. "Expropriation of Foreign Investment: Summary of the Post World War II Experience of American and British Investors in the Less Developed Countries." *Journal of International Business Studies,* Fall.

Tugendhat, Christopher. 1972. *The Multinationals.* New York: Random House.

United Nations. 1956–70. *Yearbook of National Accounts Statistics.* New York: Department of Economic and Social Affairs, Statistical Office.

U.S. Department of Commerce, Bureau of the Census. 1966. *1963 Census of Manufacturers, Survey and Subject Statistics.* Washington, D.C.: U.S. Government Printing Office.

U.S. Congress, Senate. 1966. Subcommittee on Anti-Trust and Monopoly of the Commission on the Judiciary. *Concentration Ratios in Manufacturing Industries 1963,* 89th Congress, 2nd Session.

U.S. Department of State. 1974. *Disputes Involving U.S. Foreign Direct Investment.* July 1, 1971 through July 31, 1973, Research Study, Bureau of Intelligence and Research.

Vaupel, J. W., and Curhan, Joan P. 1969. *The Making of Multinational Enterprise.* Division of Research, Harvard Graduate School of Business Administration, Boston.

————. 1973. *The World's Multinational Enterprises.* Division of Research, Harvard Graduate School of Business Administration, Boston. 1973.

Vernon, Raymond. 1971. *Sovereignty at Bay: The Multinational Spread of U.S. Enterprises.* New York: Basic Books.

_____. 1974. "Annual Progress Report, Harvard Business School Multinational Enterprise Project," 1973–74.

_____. 1974. "The location economic activity." In *Economic Analysis and the Multinational Enterprise.* Eds. J. H. Dunning. New York: Praeger, 1974.

Weigel, Dale. 1970. "Restrictions on Dividend Repatriations and the Flow of Direct Investment to Brazil." *Journal of International Business,* Fall.

Wells, Louis, ed. 1972. *The Product Life Cycle and International Trade.* Boston: Harvard Graduate School of Business.

Wilkenfield, Jonathan. 1974. "Conflict Linkages in the Domestic and Foreign Spheres." *Quantitative Analysis of Political Data.* Ed. Samuel Kirkpatrick. Columbus, Ohio: Charles Merrill.

World Handbook of Political and Social Indicators II. 1971. Codebook sections II–IV: Events: Ann Arbor Michigan: Inter-university Consortium for Political Research.

World Handbook of Political and Social Indicators. 1972. Eds. C. L. Taylor and M. C. Hudson. New Haven: Yale University Press, 2nd edition.

Zink, Dolph Warren. 1973. *The Political Risks for Multinational Enterprise in Developing Countries.* New York: Praeger.

LARS H. THUNELL is an international financial analyst for Business International Corporation, New York, N.Y. and a contributing editor to the company's weekly *Business International Money Report.*

Before joining Business International Mr. Thunell was a Research Fellow at the Center for International Affairs, Harvard University. There he did research on the investment behavior of international firms, using the Multinational Enterprise Project databank at the Harvard Business School. This research constitutes the basis for this book.

Mr. Thunell has also been Research Associate at the Swedish Center of International Affairs in Stockholm and has held various teaching and administrative positions at the Department of Political Science, University of Stockholm. As a consultant to the Swedish Defense Planning Board he completed a study of how increasing economic interdependence among nations and the growth of multinational corporations might influence Swedish security policy. Mr. Thunell will receive his Ph.D. from the University of Stockholm in May 1977.

LABOR PRACTICES OF U.S. CORPORATIONS IN SOUTH AFRICA
Desaix Myers III

MULTINATIONAL CORPORATIONS AND GOVERNMENTS: Business-Government Relations in an International Context
edited by Patrick M. Boarman and
Hans Schollhammer

THE NATION-STATE AND TRANSNATIONAL CORPORATIONS IN CONFLICT: With Special Reference to Latin America
edited by Jon P. Gunnemann

NATIONAL CONTROL OF FOREIGN BUSINESS ENTRY: A Survey of Fifteen Countries
Richard D. Robinson

*MANAGING MULTINATIONAL CORPORATIONS
Arvind V. Phatak

*Also available in paperback as a PSS Student Edition